PHILADELPHIA SPIRITUALISM AND
the Curious Case
OF KATIE KING

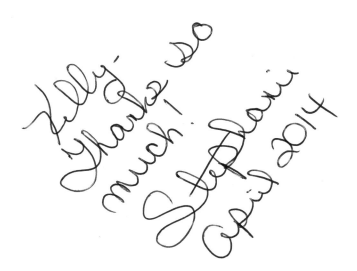

Kelly—
Thanks so
much!
Stephanie
April 2014

PHILADELPHIA SPIRITUALISM *and* the Curious Case *of* KATIE KING

STEPHANIE HOOVER

Charleston THE History PRESS London

Published by The History Press
Charleston, SC 29403
www.historypress.net

First published 2013

Manufactured in the United States

ISBN 978.1.62619.153.2

Library of Congress CIP data applied for.

To my cross-country son, who has more courage than I could ever muster.

To my husband, whose loyalty and support will always amaze me.

To my mother, who taught me the value of hard work.

To my father's spirit, wherever it may be. Your little girl turned out OK.

Contents

Acknowledgements

I CAN'T IMAGINE ever writing book acknowledgements without first thanking the staff of the Pennsylvania State Library. Whether finding a lost roll of newspaper microfilm or suggesting an obvious resource I blindly overlooked, these folks are worth far more than their salaries and deserve far more than this simple thank-you. As Walter Cronkite once said, "Whatever the cost of our libraries, the price is cheap compared to that of an ignorant nation."

Although mine was likely a sensitive topic for them (no pun intended), I am exceedingly impressed by and thankful for the prompt responses from the professional mediums of Lily Dale, New York, whom I contacted while researching this book. I cannot testify to their supernatural abilities, but I can assure you that, as human beings, they are attentive, respectful and helpful.

Many thanks also to the members of the LinkedIn Port City Paranormal Group—especially Jane, William and Doug—who offered great suggestions for research and whose serious contemplation of the field of paranormal study should serve as an example to others.

Lastly, a nod to my own "inner circle" who convinced me that my first book wasn't just a fluke. This second book wasn't any easier to write, but it was an absolute joy to complete.

Introduction

DO YOU BELIEVE we can return to earth in spirit form after death? More importantly, some readers may ask, does the author believe in life after death?

To answer the latter question, I can only say that this book is not about *my* experiences or opinions; rather, it explores the reasons why some of us so easily yield to the possibility of the supernatural and why others so guiltlessly profit from it.

In 1817, poet Samuel Taylor Coleridge begged of his readers "that willing suspension of disbelief…which constitutes poetic faith." Simply put, he was asking his audience to embrace the impossible. To abandon all rules of reason. He demanded this concession because Coleridge knew his readers could only enjoy his fantastical stories if they gave themselves permission to fully escape into his fiction.

Psychiatrists regard the suspension of disbelief as a form of regression—a return to developmental infancy when we possess no filter for what is logical and what is infeasible. But the fact is, humans need the ability to suspend disbelief. How else could we lose ourselves in a sci-fi movie, laugh at cartoons or sit wide-eyed through a magic show? Surely there is no danger in this acquiescence, for we know when to free our minds and when to rein them in. But what happens if we choose *not* to return to the land of logic?

Usually we are forcibly dragged back to reality by spouses, bosses or any one of the countless other mundane influences that constitute this life mortal. On rare occasion, however, we successfully lose ourselves in the company of individuals who cultivate and perpetuate our continued delusion because it benefits *them*. Numbered among this company were many Spiritualists of the Victorian era.

Most social and religious movements lack a precise conception date. Not so with Spiritualism. What would become a worldwide phenomenon attracting some of the most influential men and women of their day started in the rustic home of an unsophisticated family in Hydesville (near Rochester), New York, on March 31, 1848. The Fox sisters had no time to regret the attention their prank (meant only to frighten their superstitious mother) soon generated, for as soon as neighbors and newspapers expressed an interest in the odd events happening at their little cottage, an elder member of the family—one who immediately smelled profit—took the children on tour. Barely educated products of a backwoods hamlet, the girls would soon become the most sought-after Spiritualist mediums in the world and the birth mothers of a new theology based on the barest speck of evidence, either earthly or paranormal.

The America of the nineteenth century proved a particularly friendly environment for the growth of Spiritualism. Just three months before the "Rochester Rappings," the cry of *Gold!* was heard at Sutter's Mill in California. The boomtown became a boom nation. This, the thousands of immigrants who flocked to the mines believed, was the land of glittering streets where anything was possible.

Like gold dust sifting through mesh screens, new cultural influences leached into communities large and small. This exposure to previously unencountered ethnic and religious creeds and philosophies helped fuel a theological controversy. Members of the rapidly growing Universalist Church of America questioned the chiefly white European belief system, which guaranteed salvation to only a few. The once sacrosanct subjects of God, heaven and the afterlife were openly debated, as were new scientific postulations about evolution and the origin of man. This American crisis of faith was only compounded by the horror of the greatest loss of life on domestic soil.

More than 600,000 men died during or as a result of the Civil War. Millions of parents, brothers, sisters and widows searched for some meaning in this immense loss. Some searched for the very meaning of life itself. What was the purpose of it if it could end so brutally—so soon? Where did the souls of loved ones go? Did they survive on some metaphysical plane accessible to mediums like the Fox sisters? And if these two young girls could commune with the dead, who else possessed this same power?

Katie King was just one of the thousands of materialized spirits that mediums, in exchange for gifts of jewelry and money and flowers, called forth from their "spirit cabinets." Katie was—at least at first—flawless in her capacity to gain the confidence of her circle of sitters. This was partly due to the fact that the American spirit of Katie King was somewhat of a sequel to the London Katie King who had so captivated such respected personages as the novelist Florence Marryat Ross Church and scientist Sir William Crookes. Katie's miraculous cross-Atlantic Philadelphia debut was therefore met with joyous acceptance by American Spiritualists undaunted by the reportage of dubious British newspapers and threats of legal action by even less amused Crown prosecutors.

Appearing at the séances of trance mediums Nelson and Jennie Holmes, Katie King enthralled her audiences while successfully blinding her devotees to the obvious impracticalities of her materialization and interaction with the living. The now famous line from *The Wizard of Oz* seems entertainingly apropos: "Pay no attention to that man behind the curtain!" Unlike the wizard's incredulous visitors, however, Katie's followers did what she told them.

In 1874, Katie King was known throughout the nation. Word of her Philadelphia séances spread across the country in both open-minded Spiritualist publications and more scrutinizing mainstream newspapers. Political cartoonists lampooned elected officials using Katie King parodies. The song written by Katie's most ardent believers became fodder for mockery. But of course she had a large and vocal band of supporters as well. Vice President Henry Wilson made a special trip to Philadelphia to sit in the darkened parlor housing the cabinet out of which Katie materialized. Legislator and reformer Robert Dale Owen defended Katie's authenticity to the detriment of his own reputation and health. Other mediums staunchly defended the Holmeses and marveled at the power they must possess to call and control a spirit as old and as mystical as Katie King.

Many Philadelphians viewed Spiritualists as a new and harmless form of entertainment. Others who might normally dismiss such things outright instead prayed for Katie King to be real. If she *were* a true spirit, perhaps she could help find little Charley Ross, the Germantown child today regarded as the victim of the nation's first kidnapping for ransom. Still others, such as the members of the Seybert Commission formed by the University of Pennsylvania, regarded Katie and her ilk as something befitting of study if not the benefit of the doubt.

In the end, while Spiritualism survives (albeit as a small and quirky congregation of believers), Philadelphia's Katie King is nearly completely forgotten. After all, suspension of disbelief is, by its very nature, only a temporary state.

Chapter 1
Foxes, Fish and the Birth of Spiritualism

Dr. Kane, of the Arctic Expedition, is soon to be married to Miss Margaretta Fox, the second of the Fox girls, who formerly resided in Rochester, New York, where they commenced the spiritual manifestations known as the "Rochester Rappings." During his absence, Miss Fox, his said-to-be-affianced, has been attending a young ladies' school in Philadelphia.
—Rochester Union, *October 1855*

ELISHA KENT KANE, Arctic explorer. It was this phrase that nearly every reporter, biographer and admirer used to describe this son of Philadelphia aristocracy.

Kane was not physically imposing, nor was he ever a healthy, robust man, yet he feared neither adventure nor risk. Before his thirty-fifth birthday, he circumnavigated the globe and traveled, often on foot, throughout India, Africa, Europe, South America and the Pacific islands. Twice he trekked the Arctic searching for another lost explorer. In the process, he reached the highest altitude man had ever achieved, and it is for this bravery he is most remembered.

Kane's fame and feats were no surprise to his family. His father, the Honorable John K. Kane, presided over Pennsylvania's Eastern District Court for more than a decade. Ignoring the virulent sentiments of a liberal press and growing Abolition Party, the elder Kane was decried for his proslavery decisions. Elisha's maternal grandfather, Thomas Leiper, was a Revolutionary War hero who, with Robert Morris, lent a portion of his fortune (earned in the exportation of tobacco) to the Bank of North America so it could, in turn, finance Washington's march to Yorktown.

The Kanes' Philadelphia estate, Fern Rock, sat on Old York Road between the city and nearby Germantown. Distinguished neighbors included the British actress and abolitionist Fanny Kemble and suffragette Lucretia Mott.

The Kanes were a serious family and one of great means. E.K. Kane was not only expected to properly represent this dignified line, he was meant to propagate it. What he was *not* meant to do was develop an infatuation for a much younger girl who professed to commune with the dead.

MARGARETTA FOX'S AGE and birth date vary widely depending on the newspaper article, book or biography you happen to read. The obvious intent of most tellings of the events that came to be known as the "Rochester Rappings" is to paint Margaretta and her sister Catharina as very young and guileless innocents swept up in the fame and hysteria generated by their prank-turned-theology. The truth, however, is likely contained in the 1850 census, which was taken before the girls became national celebrities—before they, their parents or older sister worked out reasons to hide the girls' true ages.

Biographical sketches, including Margaretta's own, had her as young as nine years old at the time of her first encounter with spirits. But the census shows that she was fourteen in 1848 and therefore fifteen at her first for-profit public séance. Catharina was two years her junior. Still children, certainly—but old enough to understand dishonesty and the impact of their actions.

Unlike their older siblings, David and Leah, who were born in New York, the two youngest girls were born in Canada. In December 1847, the Fox family moved into a plain home in Hydesville, Wayne County, New York—a town more recently known as Arcadia. Prior to the infamy wrought by the Fox sisters, Wayne County was best known as the birthplace of Mormonism. Joseph Smith Jr. owned a farm in Palmyra, a small town just west of Hydesville, and it is here where he purportedly received a visit from both God and Jesus, an event he came to call the First Vision. Less than ten years later, in 1830, a local printer published the first Book of Mormon. The publication site is today maintained by the Church of Latter-Day Saints and operates as both historical landmark and tourist destination.

The Fox home, like most in Hydesville, was built to house laborers and farmers. It was an unassuming two-story cottage carved into a kitchen, sitting room and two bedrooms: one for the girls and one for the parents. Windows, somewhat of a luxury at the time, were few.

Margaretta's father, John D. Fox, was a blacksmith until middle age and a farmer toward the end of his life. Born in New York and of German heritage, John was described by intimates as intemperate and by biographers as devout. Margaret Fox, John's wife, was a large woman with a double chin and ample bosom whose hair was covered as her religion dictated. According to Margaretta's later accounts, it was her mother who frequented the Methodist church and in fact separated from John several times due to his drinking.

John and Margaret's son David, the eldest child, lived in a nearby home with his own wife and family. The second-oldest child, Leah, married and was then deserted by a man named Fish. Although nearly all versions of the Fox girls' story (including Margaretta and Catharina's) insist that Leah was more than twenty years older than her sisters, the census proves this to be untrue. David was born in 1820. Leah (more accurately, Ann Leah) was born in 1821, making her only thirteen years older than Margaretta. Certainly, this age difference—and Leah's more distant residence—likely worked against any close relationship among the sisters. Upon her husband's unexpected departure several years earlier, Leah had moved to Rochester (the closest "big town"), where she supported herself and her daughter, Elizabeth, by teaching music lessons.

Of the three sisters—Leah, Margaretta (commonly known as Maggie) and Catharina (who went by Katie, not to be confused with our subject Katie King)—Maggie was the most feminine and petite. The brown hair she parted in the middle and pulled back in a bun at the nape of her neck accentuated her fair skin, large, dark eyes and small mouth. Though Katie wore the same hairstyle, the effect was less flattering, for it made even more prominent her long, sharp nose, the bulb of which pointed down toward her squared chin. Leah was a less pleasing, more masculine version of Maggie with eyes hooded by low, heavy brows.

Maggie and Katie's education was short and rudimentary. Like many bored but creative children, the sisters worked hard to amuse themselves. Soon after moving to the Hydesville home, the girls discovered that thumping an apple on their bedroom floor greatly perplexed their mother, who could never ascertain from exactly where the sounds originated. When in her bedroom, Mrs. Fox thought the sounds were made by footsteps on the stairs. When heard from downstairs, the thuds seemed to come from inside the walls.

The noises were particularly troubling at night, and though Mrs. Fox repeatedly searched the house—including the girls' bedroom—no source could be found. Maggie and Katie were quite clever in hiding their culpability. Shortly after initiating the apple prank, they learned that if a string was tied to the stem, the apple could be quickly snatched up and hidden in the bedcovers, the one area their parents never examined.

Although both Fox girls took credit, it was their cousin Elizabeth Fish who first realized she needed no other instrument than her own body to create unusual sounds. One night while visiting the Fox home, she pushed against the footboard of the bed with her feet and, to everyone's surprise, created loud "pops" as the joints in her toes stretched open. Not to be outdone, the Fox sisters experimented and practiced until they could manipulate the joints in their toes at will. The resulting sharp rapping sounds were particularly loud when Maggie and Katie stood barefoot on the floor. Like a modern amplifier, the wood served to broadcast the rapping while shielding the actual source of the sound. By March 1848, Mrs. Fox was so troubled by the strange, untraceable noises permeating her home that she insisted the girls sleep in her bedroom. This news must have tickled the sisters, whose efforts now shifted into overdrive.

March 31, 1848, marked the third night of the girls' toe rapping and surreptitious finger snapping. Although originating just feet away from their parents, the taps and thuds seemed to emanate from all corners of the cottage. It was on this night, when their mother had reached her wits' end, that the children decided to take their joke one step further: they decided to communicate with the "unknown" force, which, though their mother seemed unsurprised, they had already named.

"Mr. Splitfoot," instructed Katie, "do as I do." She clapped her hands. An equal number of raps sounded in response.

Katie clapped again. Again, this was followed by an equal number of knocks.

Maggie and Katie watched with delight as their gullible mother grew more flummoxed and agitated. It was, after all, their mother for whom the whole hoax had been perfected. But what Katie did next would turn their childish lark into a worldwide theological phenomenon. It was such a simple thing—perhaps that's why it took a child to think of it. Katie *spoke* to the imaginary Mr. Splitfoot. To be more accurate, she asked him a question: "Are you a human or a spirit?"

"A spirit," came the response. It was the rap heard 'round the world. And so it happened that on this night, March 31, 1848, Modern Spiritualism—the belief in the ability of the living to speak to the dead—was born.

Never before in history had a movement based on so little evidence (some say none at all) been so enthusiastically received by so many people. And

Spiritualism was born on March 31, 1848, when Katie Fox (left) and Maggie Fox (middle) first purportedly communicated with the spirit of a dead former resident of their Hydesville, New York home. From *Hydesville in History.*

never before had a clever ruse perpetrated by teenage girls resulted in the deception of so many faithful adherents.

Stories of ghosts and haunted houses have been debated if not believed by men throughout the ages, and every religion hinges on a belief in one or more spirits. *Speaking* with the dead, however...surely it was impossible, perhaps even heretical. But that was before the Fox girls and their mysterious rappings.

Once Maggie and Katie convinced their mother they were indeed speaking to a departed soul, they began asking questions about his life and how he died. Through a complex series of knocks, the girls relayed the story of a man in his thirties who professed he was murdered in the house and buried in the cellar. While mortal, he said, he had a wife and five children but his spouse had since died.

Mrs. Fox's fear was trumped by her astonishment at her daughters' ability. She called the neighbors to witness these miraculous events for themselves, and they, of course, asked their own questions to test the spirit's veracity.

The Fox cottage was moved to the Spiritualist community of Lily Dale, New York, in 1916. It was destroyed by a fire in 1955. From *Hydesville in History.*

The accurately rapped responses were shocking and frightening but also seductive to those called to watch. Though the girls didn't realize it, they were performing the first public séance.

The buzz that spread through Hydesville grew until it filled the county and eventually the state. Within weeks, newspaper headlines touted the strange happenings at the little Fox cottage and the ability of two young girls to speak to the dead.

When Ann Leah Fox Fish learned of her sisters' "gift," she was intrigued. But unlike the strangers who willingly accepted these activities as paranormal, Leah suspected the source was far more mundane—although profitable either way. She traveled the thirty miles to Hydesville to investigate and uncover her sisters' secrets. They willingly complied, even going so far as to teach Leah the trick of popping the joint in her big toe. Leah eventually succeeded in producing sound but never became as adroit as her younger siblings. It didn't matter, however, because Leah's bent was more promoter than performer. She returned to Rochester with Katie. Maggie briefly went to live with a family friend named E.W. Capron, a newspaperman who eventually assumed publicity duties for the family.

Less than a year after what came to be called "the miracle at Hydesville," Leah arranged for the first exhibition of the Fox girls' paranormal talent at Corinthian Hall in Rochester. Rather than the shorter dresses girls their age would normally wear, Leah costumed them in full-length gowns to hide their feet. The amount of fabric required in the manufacture of the garments prompted one observer to note that the girls "ought to have been attended by a train bearer."

The event was billed as the first live demonstration of "mediumship," a bridging of the gap between the earthly and spiritual realms. Some audience members accepted the girls as genuine the second the rapping began. Others—particularly those with strong, traditional religious roots—were angered to the point of hostility. Proving that old adage that all publicity is good publicity, however, the Fox girls were soon touring throughout New York and nearby states.

In her greed, Leah accomplished several firsts of her own. She was the first promoter to charge the audience an admission fee to see mediums perform. She also later initiated the practice of charging attendees of private séances and circles.

Maggie and Katie, shepherded by Leah and sometimes accompanied by their mother, booked rooms at hotels where guests came to ask questions of and about departed loved ones. Some events were chaotic with all three Fox women rapping in response to questions, the upside of which was that nearly any answer could be claimed correct. And from very early on, however, there were skeptics who sought to prove the performances fraudulent.

In May 1850, a sad young man called upon the Fox sisters. In his hat was a weed signifying the mourning of the passing of someone dear. In a voice choked with emotion, he asked if he could be put in contact with his departed mother. After a few moments of silence, a knock was heard. It is your mother, the young man was assured, and he dabbed his teary eyes with his handkerchief.

"Where are you, Mother? Are you happy?" he asked.

Raps sounded. "Yes," Leah translated. "She is happy. Her spirit is at rest."

"Are your friends with you?" the grieving son wondered.

"Oh yes," Leah said. "Your mother can see her friends anytime she wishes."

Seemingly satisfied, the young man rose and returned his hat to his head. Before leaving, he turned to the Fox sisters. In a quiet voice he said, "I have been very much entertained, as no doubt my mother herself will be, for I left her at home not half an hour since basting a turkey for dinner."

IN THE FALL of 1852, Maggie and her mother booked a room in Webb's Union Hotel on Arch Street in Philadelphia. They arrived in the city to offer personal receptions with those wishing to investigate spiritual manifestations. Although Maggie said she was "scarcely thirteen," in actuality she was

Famed Arctic explorer and Philadelphia native Elisha Kent Kane tried to save Maggie Fox from a lifetime of deceiving others in the name of Spiritualism, but he died just before the couple was to be married. From *Biography of Elisha Kent Kane*.

eighteen years of age when Elisha Kent Kane happened upon her in one of the bridal parlors reserved for the Foxes' sittings. Whether or not he knew her true age is unclear, but it appears most likely that he was, like so many of Maggie's acquaintances, deceived.

For Kane it was love—or, at the very least, brotherly affection—at first sight. He never for a moment, however, believed that Maggie or anyone else in her family actually communicated with the dead. The sideshow that had become Maggie's life both saddened and angered him. He instantly recognized her intelligence and promise and, soon after cultivating a personal relationship with her, demanded that she quit Spiritualism and move into the home of his aunt. There in Philadelphia, she would be educated and cultured and kept chaste until he returned to marry her. That Maggie complied with these requests is tantamount to a confession of her complicity in the sham the Fox sisters instigated and perpetrated. Sadly, however, Elisha Kent Kane died shortly after their engagement announcement appeared in newspapers. It was a personal loss, surely, and the end of any chance she had at security or normalcy. To survive, Margaretta Fox returned to performing the rapping séances she and her sisters introduced to the world. She would, by turns, defend and renounce Spiritualism for the rest of her life.

Chapter 2

Philadelphia's Spiritualists

IN 1838, AN ITINERANT preacher named Thomas H. Stockton arrived in Philadelphia with the goal of establishing the First Methodist Protestant Church there. To house his forthcoming flock, he secured a well-maintained but plain building on Third Street in the Northern Liberties section of the city. Owing to the church's seating capacity of one thousand, it seems he had high hopes for his mission, and at first this optimism seemed merited. But after nine years of struggling to win the faith of an apathetic populace, Stockton moved westward to Ohio in 1847, leaving the building untenanted.

In this same year, Andrew Jackson Davis authored (or, according to him, dictated while in a trance) a three-part book called *The Principles of Nature, Her Divine Revelations, and a Voice to Mankind.* Predating the recognized birth of Spiritualism by a year, Davis's composition described in lengthy detail his belief that spirits, once freed from mortal constraints, could achieve possession of all knowledge of both the material and ethereal universe. By extracting this knowledge, Davis proposed, harmony between all religions, cultures and people could be cultivated.

The work created considerable interest in Philadelphia, where a committee was formed in the autumn of 1850 to read the book publicly. Shortly thereafter, the book's readers consulted a clairvoyant medium who directed them on the creation of circles through which communication with spirits could be established. Although the circles met regularly for four months, nothing happened. On February 1, 1851, the spirits broke their silence.

Andrew Jackson Davis was a nineteenth-century clairvoyant whose book inspired Philadelphia Spiritualists to form the first circle in that city. Image, circa 1847, of unknown origin.

The first well-defined communication between a Philadelphia circle and the dead was made through a series of raps—exactly as the Fox sisters of Hydesville, New York, had described. Within three weeks, raps were heard in two other areas of the city with the aid of other mediums. The resulting wave of public interest precipitated the need for a headquarters for the original committee members, and soon the former Stockton church was home to the First Association of Spiritualists in Philadelphia.

Stockton would likely have been both appalled and envious. Unlike his own church, no proselytizing, cajoling or guilt was required to entice Spiritualists—they simply came. Stockton's church was soon known by another moniker: Harmonial Hall, a nod to Davis's book and philosophy. It held seven lectures and conferences per week in total, including two on Sunday.

Less than ten years after the Fox girls first rapped with the dead, a Catholic council calculated there to be three million Spiritualists nationwide. Twenty years after the Rochester Rappings, an estimated three hundred mediums operated in Philadelphia (six hundred elsewhere in Pennsylvania), and no fewer than sixteen circles met regularly in private residences. These meetings were typically invitation only (by the mediums running them), and like the overwhelming majority of the supporters of this new religious philosophy, these circle sitters included some of the most well educated and well-to-do residents of the Quaker City.

ROBERT HARE WORKED much of his life as a professor of chemistry at the University of Pennsylvania. He was born in Philadelphia and, when barely past his teen years, inherited a large brewery from his English father. Hare's tenure as brewmaster was brief, for his interest in scientific pursuits exceeded his business acumen. Hare's significant contributions to the field of chemistry include the invention of the oxyhydrogen blowtorch, the development of the voltaic battery and a method for denarcotizing laudanum.

Hare was a robust man. Thick, wavy hair crowned his large head, and a low-set beard belted his chin. By all accounts, he was affectionate but prone to the distraction that results when the human brain attempts far too many calculations at once.

Hare's first contacts with Spiritualists were born of skepticism. In 1853, he began testing mediums to stem the tide of what he called the "gross delusion called Spiritualism." To aid in this effort, he invented a machine he dubbed the Spiritoscope, a device meant to allow the living to speak to the spirits without the

Robert Hare was a noted scientist who set out to prove mediums as frauds but soon became an outspoken supporter of Spiritualism. From *Popular Science Monthly*.

medium as middleman. Another of his inventions predated but functioned similarly to Ouija boards. Hare called it a Psychograph to lend it a scientific aura, but the contraption bore a striking resemblance to a carnival wheel of chance. Numbers and letters of the alphabet rimmed the wheel, allowing mediums—supposedly under the physical control of spirits—to start and stop the oversized dial to spell out answers.

The more mediums Hare visited (and the more familiar they became with his life story), the more amazing their powers seemed and the more convinced he became of their legitimacy. By 1854, Hare was an openly devout Spiritualist who wrote several books on the subject, including his most famous, *Spiritualism Scientifically Demonstrated*.

For his former Harvard and Yale chums, even *testing* Spiritualists implied that their humbuggery might have credence, and early on these old friends publicly disparaged Hare. The American Association of the Advancement of Science, which once praised and honored him, sought retraction of Hare's membership. Hare did tone down public statements about Spiritualism and religion, although he privately maintained belief in mediums until his death in 1858. Despite his attempt to distance himself,

Hare would forever be associated with this theology, as proved by the final sentence of his obituary in the *Scientific American*: "In his old age he became a convert to spiritualism—this being the single instance, so far as we are aware, of a man who had been trained to original scientific investigation, becoming the subject of this wonderful delusion."

Of all of Philadelphia's Spiritualists, none was as certain of its credibility as Henry Seybert. Not only was he an avid supporter and believer, Seybert was also a very wealthy man whose last will and testament provided for a professorial position at the University of Pennsylvania on the condition that a commission to study Spiritualism be impaneled.

Henry's father, Adam, was an eminently respected chemist and mineralogist and an eight-term congressman representing Philadelphia. Henry's mother died in childbirth, leaving Adam as the sole caregiver of the infant, and the two remained intensely bonded throughout their lives. Adam died in Paris in 1825 with Henry by his side. Adam's death was devastating to his only child, who, at twenty-three, became the sole beneficiary of his father's estate estimated at $300,000—more than $7 million by today's valuation.

Henry Seybert had always considered himself a Christian and accepted the bargain of belief in things unseen in return for salvation. The death of his father, however, precipitated a crisis of faith with which he would struggle for two decades. It also left him with a fortune that, rather than engendering gratitude, plagued him with fear and guilt. He knew well the biblical warning: it is easier for a camel to pass through the eye of a needle than a rich man to enter the gates of heaven. The prospect of eternal damnation tortured him. Seybert sought conference with religious scholars who assured him this verse served as an admonition to the *sinful* rich—not charitable men like himself and not the wealthy who wisely resisted the lure of materialism and excess.

As Spiritualism attracted more and more devotees, Seybert—like others of his well-educated friends and colleagues—sought to learn why. For him, the answer was rooted in its simplicity. Unlike Christianity, which demanded unquestioning servitude, Spiritualism demanded only that followers suspend disbelief. This Seybert did with energetic conviction.

In December 1882, in a strong and legible hand, Henry Seybert wrote a lengthy, detailed will. The bequest best remembered promised $60,000 to the University of Pennsylvania if it would create a commission of open-minded men to impartially investigate Spiritualism and the mediums who practiced it. When Seybert died the following March, the university endeavored to honor his final wishes. Those who knew Seybert were relieved that he did not live to read the findings.

THOMAS R. HAZARD came often to Philadelphia to participate in séances, but he never considered staying. Even the call of Spiritualism could not separate Hazard from Vaucluse, his Rhode Island colonial-inspired estate. With its boxwood labyrinth and guesthouses nestled among the trees bounding the property, Vaucluse was Hazard's refuge. In it survived the memories of his departed wife and later the four daughters, the lights of his life, taken by tuberculosis before their fortieth birthdays.

Neighbor Florence Howe Hall remembered Hazard as an affable but gullible friend. Once, she reported in her autobiographical work *Memories Grave and Gay*, her family and Hazard's went to a performance of the magician Elbert Anderson. Hazard was convinced Anderson's tricks were truly supernatural and that they could only work with the aid of the spirits. After prolonged argument and persuasion, the other members of the party convinced Hazard the magician's act was simple human chicanery. Hazard may have changed his mind about Anderson, but he assured his friends, "Just such things are done by Spiritualists."

His conviction that Spiritualism was a real conduit between the living and the dead never faltered—even after police broke in to a séance he was attending and arrested a medium on charges of fraud while "materializing" the face of one of Hazard's daughters.

Mrs. Hardy was famous for wax face molds similar to these, supposedly physical proof of her ability to call forth the spirits of the dead. From *Confessions of a Medium*.

DR. HENRY T. CHILD retained his good name until the end of his life, although he was far more outspoken and active in Spiritualism than was Hare. Child was born in Philadelphia's Northern Liberties, and it would be his only place of permanent residence. He was the son of Quakers, benefited from a Quaker education and both accepted and advocated for the Friends' belief in abolition of slavery, gender equality and charitable works. Child always assumed he would follow his father in the clock-making trade, but the summer of 1832 would forever alter his plans.

Ships arriving in the ports of Philadelphia, New York, Portsmouth and Norfolk that July carried more than just thousands of immigrants. The cholera bacteria that had ravaged the Asian continent, particularly India, found passage as well. After a brief summer respite with no new cases, the Cholera Board of Philadelphia was hopeful that the city had been spared the worst. Unlike in previous epidemics, it took proactive measures. As soon as cases were reported in other eastern cities, Philadelphia officials ordered the streets to be swept and rinsed of human and animal waste and other filth. They erected ten temporary hospitals specifically outfitted to combat cholera. The board assured newspaper reporters these facilities were well supplied, well ventilated and fully staffed. "There exists no panic among the citizens," the *Philadelphia Gazette* reported in early August.

But within days, hospitals were again treating cholera patients, six of whom died. On August 12, more than one hundred new cases were reported. On August 30, forty-eight more Philadelphians contracted the disease.

As the summer wore on, the cholera pandemic became more virulent, spreading across the United States and Europe. Residents of Philadelphia ran to nearby counties and states, where they succeeded only in spreading the contagion. Before it was fully contained, more than 150,000 Americans succumbed to the disease—nearly 1,000 of them in Philadelphia. Among the dead were Child's two brothers. He and his father both contracted cholera but survived. The teenager wondered if his life's work should be healing people rather than repairing clocks.

At the age of twenty-one, Child married Quakeress Anna R. Pickering. She died only a year into their marriage. The couple's infant daughter died shortly afterward. By age twenty-four, when he entered into the study of medicine, Child had suffered more loss than most suffer in a lifetime. When, in 1851, he learned of the beliefs espoused by Spiritualists—particularly the comforting conviction that the spirit has an unbroken and continual existence—Child quickly and completely immersed himself in the movement. Like Robert Hare, he likely would have been a lifelong disciple of Spiritualism. Unlike Hare, however, Child had the misfortune of meeting Katie King.

ROBERT DALE OWEN was not a Philadelphia native, nor did he own a home in the city. But when news of the amazing séances of Nelson and Jennie Holmes reached him in Indiana, he took up temporary residence there to witness firsthand the materializations of Katie King.

Owen's father, who also went by Robert but no middle name, was a cotton manufacturer in New Lanark, Scotland. In addition to implementing labor reforms that benefited his own employees, the elder Owen waged public battles against class distinctions and theological dogmas held dear by his contemporaries. In 1824, he came to America to found New Harmony, Indiana. This utopian community was

Robert Dale Owen was a politician and liberal social activist who became a particularly popular (and easy) target among non-Spiritualists. His affection for and loyalty to Katie King would only tarnish a fine career. From *Pioneers of Birth Control in England and America.*

based on the town of Harmony in Butler County, Pennsylvania. Both touted the concepts of communal living and equal distribution of the food and material goods residents produced. New Harmony was a failure in Indiana, and Owen returned home, where he lived out his life doing charitable works, promoting "reasonable" religious views and advocating improved working conditions.

Robert Dale Owen was born in Glasgow, Scotland, on November 7, 1801. He was with his father during the birth and failure of New Harmony. After its demise, the younger Owen traveled throughout Europe before returning to Indiana, where he became an American citizen in 1827. Very much his father's son, Owen—along with noted abolitionist and feminist Frances (Fanny) Wright—began publication of a newspaper called the *Free Inquirer*. The paper touted the benefits of socialism and, much in keeping with the elder Owen's convictions, questioned the supernatural elements of mainstream religions. It failed after three years.

After 1838, when Owen married Mary Jane Robinson, his political career blossomed with incredible rapidity. He was elected to the Indiana Congress, spearheaded legislative reform allowing independent ownership of land by Indiana women, appropriated funding to develop and support a statewide common school system, proposed creation of and served as regent for a national Smithsonian Institution and loudly supported emancipation of slaves.

Ten years her senior, Robert Dale Owen never entertained the possibility that Mary Jane would predecease him. On a sunny day in September 1871—well after his initiation into Spiritualism—he eulogized his wife at her graveside:

> *I do not believe more firmly in these trees that spread their shade over us, in this hill on which we stand, in these sepulchral monuments we see around us here—that I do that human life, once granted, perishes never more...I believe, as she did, in the meeting and recognition of friends in Heaven. While we mourn below there are joyful reunions above.*

Two years later, Owen was the featured speaker at an event at the Boston Music Hall commemorating the twenty-fifth anniversary of Spiritualism. Several thousand people attended, all of whom regarded him as living proof of everything good about the movement. But it was obvious that Owen was tired. His voice, barely audible, wavered on occasion. He seemed like a man for whom life was losing its wonder.

Perhaps it was the emotional weakness that comes with an advanced age; perhaps his brain—taxed for too many decades by deep and continual thought—did become "soft." Perhaps he was simply lonely for Mary Jane. Whatever the cause, Katie King would spawn in Robert Dale Owen a new vitality. She would convince him that Heaven was not the only place where he could reunite with his wife. It could just as easily be accomplished in a three-story brick apartment building in Philadelphia.

HOWEVER IT CAME to be, the characteristic shared by proponents of Spiritualism was the overwhelming need to understand what happened after death. Is there an afterlife? Are spirits immortal? Will my loved ones welcome me to eternity? Surely these questions have plagued mankind since humans first witnessed death. What was unusual about the Spiritualist movement, however, was how quickly—and easily—it turned a profit on these uncertainties. And Spiritualists were not the only opportunists.

Throughout the ages, book publishers have capitalized on trends, passions and preoccupations. Shortly after the Rochester Rappings first captivated the nation, countless books on Spiritualism appeared in bookstores. Many were written by Spiritualist supporters championing the movement. Other books were written to warn the public that a skilled medium's true talent was separating money from wallets, not reuniting the living with the dead. A not insignificant number of treatises were written by clergy from mainstream religions who decried Spiritualism as the work of Satan, a fiendish attempt to topple whichever church the writer represented and take with it the souls of its followers. Psychologists fretted in print that the delusions inspired by Spiritualism could only lead to insanity—a proposition seemingly supported by salacious newspaper reports of circle sitters' suicides and mediums descending into madness.

T.W. Evans was neither a Spiritualist nor did he set out to be a publisher, but he did recognize a good business deal when he saw one. Originally the operator of a Philadelphia perfumery, Evans expanded his shelf space to include dry goods, clothing, hardware and anything else he thought he could sell. In 1869, he published Herbert Hamilton's book, *Psychomancy, Fascination or Soul Charming*. At four hundred pages, it was a hefty tome, bound in cloth. The ads Evans ran in magazines and newspapers across the nation boasted that this was a "wonderful book [with] full instructions to enable the reader to fascinate either sex, or any animal, at will." It also promised to reveal the secrets of Spiritualists. An expanded version of the ad running in 1871 promised that the book was a perfect resource for those seeking to start a trance medium business. Evans's book—reprinted as late as 1877—sold more than 100,000 copies in its first year, some by mail but most from his Eighth Street shop. The hard-copy edition sold for $1.25. For aspiring mediums on a budget, the paperback version was just $1.00.

Samuel Barry was another accidental publisher, and it was he who distributed Robert Hare's 1855 *Lecture on Spiritualism*. Barry was also a book dealer, and his shop on Arch Street held, according to his ads, "all Spiritual products that are published." A tenant above the bookstore, T. Starr, a self-described "highly developed clairvoyant," apparently found the city less conducive to his professional goals than did his landlord. Starr's ad—running at the same time as Barry's—expressed his desire to relocate to a "pleasant country town already awakened to Spiritual manifestations."

For most of Philadelphia's mediums, Spiritualism brought nothing if not easy money, and they enjoyed their own gold rush of sorts. No sooner did a shingle or ad appear than clients begged for admittance to private circles and public showings at homes, hotels and halls throughout the city. In 1871, several dozen mediums and clairvoyants publicly advertised their services. Many offered unique specialties such as healing, trance writing, rapping and even magic. One went so far as to provide long-distance readings if a lock of hair and five dollars were remitted.

The one enterprise at which Philadelphia Spiritualists failed miserably was the publication of a periodical. Although there were nearly thirty large, successful Spiritualist publications produced around the world, Philadelphia's only entry, the *White Banner*, suffered a quick and embarrassing death. Six issues into its existence, it still had not attracted a sufficient number of readers willing to pay the dollar-per-year (or five-cents-per-issue) subscription rate, and the paper folded. It was a rude shock to the editors. Even Melbourne, Australia Spiritualists boasted a successful newspaper—perhaps not all that shocking when one considers a member of the legislature also worked as a professional medium.

White Banner aside, the enthusiasm of Philadelphia proselytes reached near fever pitch by the 1870s. Come spring of 1874, the most powerful and celebrated manifestation of all would astound and confound believers and skeptics alike.

Chapter 3
Katie King Debuts in London

HYDESVILLE SET THE SCENE for the Spiritualist movement, but it needed guiding principles upon which to grow. Unlike other religions, there was no national organization, nor was there a published canon from which to ascertain guidance. The gospel of Spiritualism was therefore established by those who practiced it:

> *First, man is a spirit, now and here.*
> *Second, man has continued existence, which the change called death does not really affect.*
> *Third, after death spirits have the power to communicate with mortals—in favorable conditions, they can even materialize.*

It was the third principle that resonated loudest with professional mediums, particularly since these mediums themselves dictated exactly what those "favorable conditions" might be.

In order to experience success in circle sittings, mediums explained, all negativity and suspicion must be banished. Anyone expressing skepticism was therefore denied entrance. With regard to the physical surroundings, the room used for the circle could be used for no other purpose, and no access by anyone but the mediums or the approved circle sitters would be granted. The sitters themselves were to occupy the same assigned seats each time.

It was, of course, pointed out that these rules seemed stacked in the medium's favor: no doubters allowed; no ability to inspect the room;

complete control over circle sitters. But, the mediums assured, these rules came from the spirits—not the mortal conduit.

But while these rules explained how the mediums established communication between the living and the dead, the question everyone wanted answered was: how did the spirit actually materialize? Mediums typically prefaced their response with a vague reference to the complexity of the subject before offering their answer. A powerful medium, they assured, can suspend the very cohesion of particles of matter composing the spirit. When the medium is finally drained by this exertion, the particles rush back to spirit land. As for the hats and adornments worn by the spirits, it was explained that when a loved one in the human sphere willed such an object to appear, the spirits obliged. Ironically, however, a spirit could never present itself to the living without shielding its body with some dense cover that protected its energy source. This is why family and friends of the departed could recognize their dead loved ones but never touch them.

Until Katie King.

It took nearly twenty years for the fire of Spiritualism to catch in England, but by the 1870s, the London Spiritualist community was large and zealous and had birthed the British National Association of Spiritualists. New mediums seemed to appear in the city daily, including Katie Fox, who married a barrister of means and started a new life outside the glare of American skeptics. Even Fox's baby boy was channeling mysterious powers and, at age five months, was writing messages from the spirits and rapping out responses with his tiny foot. From May 21, 1871, to May 21, 1874, however, the most famous medium in London was a young girl named Florence Cook.

In interviews, Florence often repeated the tale that her grandmother was a medium who, after laying in trances that sometimes lasted weeks, made accurate predictions of future events. Florence's own powers were first discovered, she said, when a schoolmate witnessed her lifting a table four feet off the ground using only telekinetic energy. In actuality, Cook had been a student of known charlatans Charles Williams and Frank Herne, who, after too many exposures of their own act, made their living "training" other mediums. It didn't take long for Cook to realize that her abilities to deceive far exceeded those of her fellow pupils, and she left Williams and Herne for her own kitchen, where she perfected her skills with her family as audience.

Perhaps she had learned about Henry Morgan in the classroom, or maybe someone else suggested she incorporate the storyline into her performance. However she happened upon it, Cook not only used the Morgan plotline,

The first Katie King as "materialized" by London's Florence Cook. From *New Light on Immortality.*

she embellished it. Shortly after stepping behind the curtain hanging in the kitchen doorway, Florence fell into a deep trance. Soon a second young woman would peek out from the drape. She introduced herself as Annie Morgan, daughter of the pirate Henry—but, she told the audience, she preferred her nickname: Katie King.

Florence's father (much like Leah Fox Fish) recognized the commercial value in his daughter's talents and soon arranged a public exhibition. Cook and King developed an immediate and loyal following. The two looked enough alike that it was easy to buy the explanation that it was only natural for Katie King to take on some of her medium's features. Yet they were different enough to reinforce the audience's belief that they were indeed two different beings: one human and the other spiritual.

Interest in Florence grew daily, and her father happily collected admission fees for her séances. When a wealthy Spiritualist patron offered a generous annuity on which Florence could comfortably live, a disappointed Mr. Cook was left to accept only the jewelry and other special gifts grateful sitters offered as thanks.

Florence Cook, the teenage medium who first materialized Katie King in London, shown here after her marriage to Elgie Corner. From *New Light on Immortality*.

Florence Cook agreed to be tested by a number of men, including noted British chemist and physicist Sir William Crookes, whose perspective was no doubted shaded by his own belief in Spiritualism. The simplest explanations—that there was a second person in the cabinet (perhaps Florence's sister) or that the entranced and motionless Florence was actually a wax doll—seemed the least considered. Instead, bizarre tests including connecting Cook to an electrical meter and tying her with wax-sealed ropes "proved" to Spiritualists that she was indeed calling forth a two-hundred-year-old revenant from the spirit world.

As with the Fox sisters, many openly opined the absurdity of Florence Cook's claims. On one occasion, a member of the audience leapt forward and grabbed "Katie"—only to encounter a struggling and very real Florence Cook, who, with great effort, eventually freed herself and fled back into her cabinet. Spiritualists were shocked and outraged at such a violation. Novelist, actress and Spiritualism devotee Florence Marryat Ross Church reported that "the medium nearly lost her life…from the sudden disturbance of the mysterious link that bound her to the spirit." Florence Cook herself denied any knowledge of the incident owing to her deep trance.

By 1880, most of England's fraudulent mediums had been exposed. It was an unfortunate year for Florence Cook as well. No longer materializing Katie King (this act had been debunked too often), Florence now materialized a spirit called "Marie." Her most embarrassing incident came when an impatient circle sitter reached inside the cabinet and tore away Marie's robes, leaving a cowering Cook garbed in nothing but underclothes.

Incredibly, Florence Cook soldiered on and lived another thirty years off the gullibility of Spiritualists. Toward the end of her life, she was invited to Poland, where her second-rate act garnered only laughter and ridicule. She died in 1904 in what would likely have been complete obscurity had it not been for two American mediums traveling abroad who saw her at the height of her popularity and brought Florence Cook's Katie King to Philadelphia.

Chapter 4

Katie King's Encore in the Quaker City

IN MAY 1874, following numerous exposures, Florence Cook announced to her London circle sitters that Katie King would no longer appear in this sphere. While most assumed "this sphere" to be the physical realm, it turned out to mean only England—for shortly before this retirement announcement, Katie King had already made her American debut.

Little is known of Nelson and Jennie Holmes outside of their involvement in the Katie King affair. They were called illiterate by some, mediums of unusual capability by others. The *Philadelphia Inquirer* suggested that their only real talent was "making the spiritualism business pay."

No public record of the couple has been found, so perhaps the surname "Holmes" was fictitious and employed to leverage the reputation of well-known Scottish medium D.D. Home, whose séances and feats of levitation were broadly reported. Whatever their biographical origins, their professional instincts told the Holmeses that "Katie King" would be warmly welcomed by the Philadelphia spiritualists who had heard stories of her miraculous materializations in London. Their instincts were right.

Nelson Holmes was described by one of his acquaintances as a slight man with effeminate gestures. Jennie, on the other hand, was characterized as a stocky, mannish woman who stood five feet and three inches tall and might have benefited from some of Nelson's delicacy. "[Jennie] is a rather prepossessing looking person," one séance attendee reported. "Her conversation showed, however, that she is not illiterate, but naturally ignorant."

The only known drawings of the pair, based on lost photographs, indicate a couple in their late thirties or early forties. Jennie's head is dominated by a mane of thick, dark curls onto which a stylish feathered hat is pinned. Nelson's hair is short at the neck and parted neatly on his right side, and his upper lip sports a mustache of a length bordering on handlebars.

Dr. Henry T. Child, who discovered the medium couple as early as April 1874, supplied their entree into Philadelphia Spiritualist society and acted as a de facto agent by personally soliciting members for their circle. On any given evening, twenty-five sitters showed up and many more were turned away at the door.

The couple rented an apartment on Ninth Street near Arch on the second floor of a stationer's shop. The circle room was sparsely furnished to allow space for that most magical of all mediums' inventions, the spirit cabinet. Made of materials ranging from simple draperies to expensive hardwood, it provided the privacy and absence of light required for manifesting the dead. The Holmeses' early spirit cabinet was somewhat rudimentary. The door to the bedroom adjoining the sitting room was opened inward toward the circle at about a sixty-degree angle. A second door, hinged to the opposite jamb, also opened inward, and where the two doors met a triangular space was formed. Into each door were cut circular openings, apertures at which spirit faces could appear. These apertures were protected by thick black curtains, for, as Nelson and Jennie explained, light hurt the materializing entities and resulted in imperfect manifestations. A board was placed atop the two doors to further create the complete darkness Nelson required.

Initially, Nelson Holmes was the main attraction. To quell any skepticism, before each sitting began visitors were invited to search the cabinet, the adjoining bedroom and Nelson himself for any props, trapdoors or accomplices. When all were satisfied that trickery seemed impossible, Jennie locked the only other entrance to the bedroom, a second doorway that emptied onto a landing.

Like Florence Cook, Holmes—once confined in his spirit cabinet— immediately fell into a trance. Usually within minutes a spirit face appeared at one of the apertures. This was typically followed by the gasp of one of the circle sitters who recognized the countenance as belonging to a family member or friend. If no one identified a face, Jennie attributed it to the spirit's inexperience at materialization. Like the living who required practice to learn new things, spirits required practice at revealing their ethereal bodies. After several more sittings, during which the returning attendees

A séance table is lifted into the air by spirits. From *Confessions of a Medium*.

revealed exactly how the spirits in the apertures differed from their loved ones, nearly all the faces were named.

Some sitters saw their wives. Others saw men with whom they had served in war. Still others saw sisters, brothers and parents. But sitters began to notice that—though bearing an obvious physical resemblance to the departed—the faces seemed consistently static. Their frozen expressions displayed but minimum human quality. In show business terms, Nelson and Jennie's act was becoming a little stale. It needed a plot twist guaranteed to set the Holmeses' circle apart from the dozens of other séances cropping up all over Philadelphia.

THE LATE 1800S were a time of great scientific discovery and debate. Andre-Marie Ampere discovered the relationship between electricity and magnetism. Christian Doppler discovered the properties of sound and light travel that came to bear his name. Joseph Lister invented the first antiseptic. Archaeologists uncovered Neanderthal fossils, and Charles Darwin introduced his theories on natural selection and the evolution of humans. The more rapidly scientific knowledge expanded, the less confident the common man was in his ability to understand it. For the devout, many of these new hypotheses flew in the face of God and religion. How could man evolve from apes? He was, after all, made in the image of the Almighty, was he not?

For all generations, paradigm shifts spark anxiety. Like those before and after them, Philadelphians sought to escape their anxiety in the theaters and halls that booked the finest performers of the day. The great Shakespearean thespian Edwin Booth captivated playgoers with his powerful oratory. Burlesque

Signor Blitz was one of the finest magicians of his day and adopted Philadelphia as his home city. While mediums may have borrowed some of his tricks and showmanship, Blitz was adamantly opposed to Spiritualists. From *The Life and Adventures of Signor Blitz*.

troupes staged outlandish extravaganzas like *The Equestrian Spectacle of Lady Godiva*, complete with Arabian horses. Comic pantomimes and song-and-dance skaters performed to large, laughing crowds. But the most popular acts were those involving magic, juggling and ventriloquism. No magician was better known in the city than Signor Blitz, a British native and Pennsylvania immigrant.

Blitz began his study of legerdemain at the age of twelve and first publicly performed at age fifteen. When his American tour brought him to Philadelphia in 1834, he forged an immediate connection with the city. He become a regular performer at a large hall at Eighth and Chestnut Streets and built a home on Wallace Street, where he lived the rest of his life.

Blitz possessed a genuine love of making people happy. He once taunted curious museum visitors by throwing his voice inside the tomb of a mummy donated by the Egyptian government. "Open the box!" the mummy seemed to cry. "Open the box!"

One brave man leaned close to the sarcophagus and asked, "What's your name?"

The magician picked his way to the front of the crowd. "Signor Blitz," he replied to thunderous applause.

During the Civil War, Blitz gave more than 130 free performances to soldiers receiving treatment in Philadelphia hospitals. It made the adopted son more beloved to the people of the city. And it demonstrated his mastery at attracting and keeping a loyal audience.

Nelson and Jennie Holmes were nothing if not fast learners. They recognized in the acts of magicians the thing they lacked most: the signature trick that could entice an audience to buy a ticket time and time again. The one most grand of finales.

One day in May, a new face appeared in the aperture of the Holmeses' spirit cabinet. It was more beautiful than any that had come before. Unlike the fixed expression worn by previous spirits, this face was lifelike. It was the face of a young woman with large gray eyes and dark hair hanging in ringlets upon her shoulders. A small, lacy veil sat atop her head.

Dr. Child barely contained his own excitement as he made the introduction. "Please meet Katie King," he said, "the materialized spirit brought forth in London by renowned medium Florence Cook."

Jennie Holmes allowed the audience to catch their breath and take in the enormity of the occasion. She then asked Katie to show the circle her hands. Katie complied, but in addition to her own, several other pairs—one clearly

A reporter's rendition of Katie King's materialization at a séance in Philadelphia. From *Frank Leslie's Illustrated Newspaper.*

that of a child—appeared in the aperture. The sitters let out a synchronized, startled chant of "Did you see that?"

"Is it true that you died over a hundred years ago?" Jennie asked the spirit.

In a smoky whisper, and with the movement of her mouth perfectly matching the spoken words, Katie replied, "Yes, and more, too." With no further prompting, she told the story of how she found herself in the Holmeses' spirit cabinet:

> *My grandfather was a well-to-do farmer in Wales who was subject to spells of insanity. We now realize he was a medium and that what we thought was madness were actually visions. My grandmother was an even more powerful medium than my grandfather. My father, John King, was born in Wales on March 17, 1636, the second of nine children. At the age of sixteen he ran away to work on a ship bound for Barbados. His mediumistic powers revealed themselves while he was at sea. At the age of nineteen, he took up the pirating life and changed his name to Henry*

Morgan. In 1659, he left the pirate life to return to London, where he married Kate Lambert. I was born of this union on May 12, 1660. A short time later, when my father's pirate bounty ran out, he returned to the sea, where he committed many dark deeds he shares not with me or anyone else. After nine years he returned to us, but he was violent and intemperate and once hit my mother, breaking her nose. He again returned

An uncredited drawing of Philadelphia's Katie King based on the only known photograph ever taken. From *Narratives of the Spirits of Sir Henry Morgan.*

to sea and in 1674 was appointed deputy governor of Jamaica by King Charles II. In 1679, he was knighted as Sir Henry Morgan, but soon after he passed into the spirit world. How surprised was he when he met me there, for unbeknownst to him, I too had passed just previously at the young age of nineteen.

As happened with Florence Cook, it appears the sitters were too awestruck to compare Katie's story with the true biography of Henry Morgan. Had they done so, they would have easily uncovered a number of flaws, not the least of which being that Morgan died in 1688, at least eight years later than Katie reported.

In answering the sitters' questions, Katie King took a decidedly American approach. When Dr. Child inquired if she would like an orange, Katie replied, "Yes, you stupid," and extended her arm through the opening to accept it. Still, her next requests implied English origins.

"Please write to Willie Harrison and tell him I am here in Philadelphia," Kate requested of Child. Harrison was the well-known editor of a London magazine called *The Spiritualist*. He also helped manage Florence Cook's nascent career before other handlers took over. "And," Katie continued, "I wish you'd write to my medium in London and tell her to come here." To prove their affinity, Kate quickly rattled off Cook's address: No. 6, Bruce Villas, Richmond Road, East London.

Secretarial assignments now concluded, Katie asked Child if he would like to touch her hair. A sharp breath escaped the sitters. Could this actually be possible?

Katie King passed a long, curled lock through the aperture for Child to hold. He told the audience it felt amazingly like fine, silky human hair.

THE HOLMESES WERE, not surprisingly, quite pleased. Their new leading lady was a runaway hit. But if they thought Signor Blitz might admire their showbiz savvy, they were wrong. Blitz, throughout his career and especially in retirement, felt a sincere need to assure audiences that his tricks were not magical but rather the product of well-practiced sleight of hand. In his autobiography, Blitz wrote:

In all my perambulations I never encountered such perverse people as the Spiritualists. Blind to the convictions of truth, and uncompromising in their belief of phenomena, they defend fiction, and emphatically ignore the Divine laws. [The] *wild and absurd scenes frequently related by those innocent of guile and imposition betray a powerful evidence of how effectually the imagination converts the senses.*

Indeed, Nelson and Jennie Holmes were the very sort of people Signor Blitz despised.

Chapter 5

The Inner Circle

THE MATERIALIZATION OF Katie King was a story too large, too viral, to be contained within the press of Philadelphia. From Milwaukee to San Francisco, from New York to St. Louis, everyone was talking about Nelson and Jennie Holmes's mediumistic miracle. The sitting room at 50 North Ninth Street was filled twice nightly at one dollar a head. Only those presenting testimonials from or introduced by friends were admitted.

There were few requests that Katie could not fulfill. If she did disappoint her sitters, the error was quickly remedied at her next materialization. Thus was the case when one audience member asked to see Katie's father, John King, alias pirate Henry Morgan. "He does not have sufficient energy to be with us tonight," Katie said. But the next night, the patriarch was prepared.

From the darkness of the spirit cabinet came the loud cry: "All hands on deck; ship ahoy!"

Sitters whispered excitedly to one another. Could it be him? When the turbaned head and swarthy face appeared in the aperture, they clapped joyously. "I am John King," he told them and then asked the audience if anyone had a spyglass. No one did, but one sitter offered opera glasses, which Jennie handed to the spirit. "I can see nothing with these," he complained before handing them back and disappearing from the aperture.

As May turned to June, the more fantastical the materializations became. On one warm Sunday evening, the spirit of Abraham Lincoln appeared, dressed all in white. He endeavored to speak but could not. The mediums explained that the vocal cords were the hardest human organs to materialize.

Abe did manage to nod in the direction of a black man seated in the front row—a gesture met with knowing smiles from the sitters.

Not all of the spirits called forth by the Holmeses were friendly. One evening a dark force calling itself Black Hawk caused even the mediums to tremble. He threw blankets in the faces of the audience and easily tossed tables and chairs about the room. Shortly after Jennie finally succeeded in coaxing Black Hawk back into the spirit cabinet, Katie stepped out in a beautiful white robe, exuding a peaceful countenance and returning the sitters to ease.

THROUGHOUT THE SUMMER of 1874, two men were a near constant presence in the Holmeses' inner circle: Dr. Henry T. Child and Robert Dale Owen. Katie rewarded their special fidelity with unique gifts. The men were allowed to take her pulse, touch her skin and place jewelry on her wrists and around her neck. Both men suffered cruel insult for their involvement in Spiritualism, but neither wilted under the attacks.

Child delivered public lectures on Katie King. He spoke of her origins in London and her marvelous ability to navigate the otherworldly waters to Philadelphia. "I have seen a great variety in the manifestations, and have had better opportunities for investigation of this phenomena than many other people. I have learned that very much depends upon the character and conditions of the persons forming the séance."

He described Katie with obvious affection and admiration. "I have never seen Katie wear the same dress on two occasions. Her wardrobe must be extensive. She always wears white, and Mr. Owen and myself have a piece of one of her dresses."

Katie even allowed Child to photograph her by the light of seven burning magnesium spirals. Although the photo quickly faded, Child was convinced he could see the wainscoting through Katie's body and dress.

Robert Dale Owen grew so close to Katie King that she addressed him as Father Owen and he, in kind, treated her like a beloved daughter. His meeting with Katie had actually been foretold by another medium, Mrs. Mary Hardy of Boston, who, on April 20, 1874, told Owen: "Before you leave the earth you shall see spectres walking about and they will take you by the hand and converse with you." When, several weeks later, word of Florence Cook reached him from London, Owen never matched it to the medium's vision. But on May 29, when he received a letter from his friend Dr. Child begging him to come to Philadelphia to see Mr. and Mrs. Holmes and their materializations of Katie King, he knew the prophecy had come true.

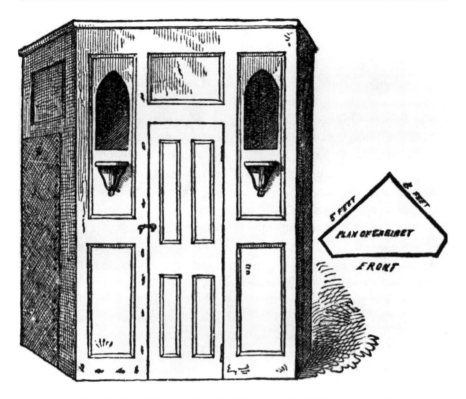

The spirit cabinet built by Nelson and Jennie Holmes for Katie King's materializations. From *People from the Other World*.

By June 5, when Owen arrived in the city, the Holmeses had upgraded their spirit cabinet from two adjoining doors with a wooden lid to a massive walnut cabinet measuring eight feet tall and seven feet wide. A single cabinet door provided access, and two apertures—five and six feet high—were curtained by dark fabric. The room itself was lowly lit, but Owen reported there was sufficient illumination to recognize the faces of several spirits.

Knowing there would be doubters, it was Katie King herself (according to Nelson and Jennie Holmes) who recommended boarding up the now unused bedroom door in front of which her new cabinet sat. This was accomplished by screwing horizontal planks of wood across the opening, creating a seemingly unbreachable barrier.

During Owen's very first visit, Katie appeared in full form—the first time she had ever done so—although she did not leave the protection of the spirit cabinet. Owen, though predisposed toward belief, regarded the materialization with some doubt. Two nights later, Katie allowed Dr. Child to measure her pulse rate of seventy-two beats per minute. One of the circle sitters offered Katie a ring and asked that Owen be the one to place it on her finger. This Katie allowed, to the hushed thrill of the attendees. "The hand was beautifully formed," a now enthralled Owen said, "like that of a mortal woman, nearly the same temperature as my own, and slightly moist."

On June 9, Owen gave Katie a chain woven from the hair of a young woman he'd once loved and had written of several years earlier in his book *The Debatable Land between This World and the Next*. Katie accepted the gift and disappeared into the cabinet. She did not return until the next evening, when she gave the chain back to Owen, telling him, "Violet wishes you to keep this, in memory of her, until you are called to meet her in spirit-home." Owen was less curious about the research that might have been conducted in Katie's absence than he was in speculating about what realm the chain may have visited during the twenty-four hours between her materializations.

Several nights later, the Holmeses held a private séance for Owen and Oluf Stenersen, Swedish envoy to the United States. After several recognizable faces appeared at the apertures, Katie King peered out and requested a pencil and paper, which one of the sitters supplied. She beckoned to Owen to come closer and gave him back the half sheet of paper with the instruction to write a private message on it. He did so and returned it to Katie, who said, "An English friend wishes to write to you." There was quiet inside the cabinet, and then a hand appeared in the aperture, one that seemingly only materialized to the wrist. It wrote on the piece of paper that seemingly floated in midair. It filled one side of the sheet with writing, turned the page over and then filled the back side. When the pencil dropped to the floor, Owen retrieved the paper from the partially materialized spirit. He found on it the three words he had written earlier, "*Ich bin hier*." But the other writing was not his. In fact, it was a letter written to Owen and signed by his friend Frederick W. Robertson.

Owen and a friend who was an expert in autographs took the sample to the Franklin Library, where they compared it against Robertson's signature in a biography. Both were convinced the letter written by the spirit was real.

On June 20, another private séance was held for Owen and his friend Mrs. L. Andrews. Owen insisted on searching the bedroom prior to the start. Both he and his friend checked under the bed, behind the door and behind the furniture. They agreed no one occupied the space. They were further advised by Nelson and Jennie that neither medium would be entering the cabinet that evening—Katie King and the other spirits were now strong enough to materialize on their own. "A remarkable sitting followed," report Owen.

THE ORIGINAL NOTE.

THE FIRST COPY.

A handwritten note from Katie King offered during one of Nelson and Jennie Holmes's Philadelphia circle sittings. From *People from the Other World*.

First, a Native American woman appeared. Then came a young boy dressed in a replicated sailor's uniform who introduced himself as Dick. At last Katie appeared, and Owen asked permission to approach her. He presented her with a mother-of-pearl cross and a note that read, "I offer you this because, though it may be simple, it is white and pure and beautiful, as you are." Katie placed the cross around her neck, kissed it and returned to her cabinet.

One evening, in what he surely believed would be a remarkable surprise, Dr. Child invited all attendees above the age of twenty to come forward to touch Katie's hand through the aperture. One of these sitters asked Katie if he might kiss her. She quickly melted back into her cabinet and returned no more that night. Owen, offended by this lack of decorum, informed Child that unless the spirits were consulted in advance of any future similar requests, he would cease his attendance at the séances. The next evening, Katie parroted these sentiments.

"Mr. Owen," she said, "indeed I cannot come out tonight unless I have assurance that my wishes shall be respected. When *you* touch me it gives me strength; but when others with whom I have no sympathy approach indiscriminately it wearies and exhausts me."

"Dear Katie," Owen assured, "I will protect you as I would my own daughter."

Several nights later, Owen was treated to a completely solitary sitting. Sauntee, the Native American princess, first appeared, and then came Katie. Owen showed her a small box he carried that contained several mementos of his meetings with her: a small card on which she'd written his name, a nosegay she gave him and a snippet of her hair. Katie asked for a pair of scissors, which were found and handed to Owen. "I will give you something truly worth keeping," she said and lowered her now uncovered head toward him. Owen cut off a four-inch ringlet. Speaking of it later, he declared, "After four months it has not melted away, and it is not distinguishable from human hair, though one seldom sees any so beautiful."

On a number of occasions, Katie levitated for the sitters. Using her hands and feet like a swimmer's, she paddled heavenward and hovered above the floor of the cabinet for ten or fifteen seconds at a time.

On July 16, Owen attended his fortieth and last séance at the home of Nelson and Jennie Holmes. He expressed sadness over his departure.

"You will return in the autumn," Katie predicted, "for I don't think that it is intended that you come to [the spirit world] yet awhile. But if [you do] be very certain that I shall be there to receive you."

Four other spirits regularly materialized at séances in the late 1800s. From *People from the Other World*.

This "spirit photograph" shows several of the subject's departed family members hovering around his head. From *The Spirit World Unmasked*.

A dead wife lovingly embraces her husband in this "spirit photograph." From *The Spirit World Unmasked*.

THOUGH OWEN AND CHILD were mocked as Katie's "chief apostles," an extraordinary number of personalities equally or more famous also sought personal audience with her. One such man was, to use the political cliché, a heartbeat away from the presidency of the United States: Vice President Henry Wilson. In one of the more unusual exchanges, Wilson asked if he might inspect Katie King's tongue, a request she honored.

Wilson's belief in Spiritualism—if indeed it ever existed—was well masked. It is known that he once posed for notorious "spirit photographer" William H. Mummer. He was also publicly outed as a Spiritualist (as were Abraham Lincoln and many others) by Warren Chase in his book *Forty Years on the Spiritual Rostrum*, although the accuracy of many of his claims is highly debatable.

That Wilson came to Philadelphia to see Katie King is a certainty. That he was convinced of her authenticity is not. Several weeks after this séance, Dr. Child found himself in the uncomfortable position of running interference for Nelson and Jennie Holmes. Responding to reports that Wilson had denounced the mediums as imposters, Child publicly replied that, while the vice president had indeed attended one of their circles, Wilson remained noncommittal in his opinion.

AUGUST 1874 PRESENTED Philadelphians with unusual weather extremes. At the start of the month, the thermometer read eighty-nine degrees in the shade. Within forty-eight hours, the temperatures fell into the low seventies. This relief was particularly welcomed by the hundreds of surveyors, laborers and mechanics constructing Memorial Hall in Fairmount Park. Built of granite and marble, Memorial Hall would be the centerpiece of Philadelphia's 1876 Centennial Exposition if it could be completed in time.

On Friday, August 7, a storm moved in from the Atlantic and stalled over southeastern Pennsylvania. More than five inches of rain fell in three days. Walls and foundations throughout the

A strange turn of events for even "spirit photography," a departed loved one appears in the belly of the individual being photographed. From *The Spirit World Unmasked.*

city weakened and shifted. Bridges gave way under tons of rushing water. Police reported several drownings. Downtown streets looked like creeks, but there was an upside: a good deal of debris and waste were washed away in advance of the nation's 100th birthday celebration. By mid-August, the temperatures again shot skyward toward the nineties, but it was, blessedly, only a brief heat wave, and the month finished with unusually cool temperatures.

The weather was not the only erratic force that summer in Philadelphia. Circle sitters invited to the apartment of Nelson and Jennie Holmes noticed unusual events there too. Though Katie King would briefly show her face or expose a slender arm through the aperture of her spirit cabinet, she would not fully materialize. Nelson said it was because a skeptic had forced his way into the cabinet and stolen all the magnetism. Jennie said that Katie was simply too weak to manifest herself, likely because of the heat, but promised that her strength would soon return.

Rumors of a more mundane fashion also circulated. Katie King, said those in the know, was on strike.

Chapter 6

Katie King Goes on the Road

WHILE KATIE KING materialized in Philadelphia, she was, for a brief time, also still appearing at the séances of Florence Cook in London. Paris boasted its own Katie King, as did a number of cities across the United States. Clearly Nelson and Jennie Holmes owned no proprietary share in their most famous manifestation.

In the fall of 1874, the mediums informed their regular sitters that they would be out of town for a while but ensured everyone Katie King would appear once again upon their return. They made a visit to Ohio and then made their way to Michigan, where Jennie had family. The Holmeses took up temporary residence in the Lyon home, where, with the assistance of Jennie's nephew—Mrs. Lyon's son—they staged séances for a fee.

Located sixty miles outside Detroit, Blissfield was a small riverfront town with a population of just 1,500. The majority of the men and women living there were practical farmers and laborers unaccustomed to, and unimpressed by, such peculiar things as clairvoyants. As in all towns they visited, however, Nelson and Jennie were enthusiastically greeted by a small group of loyal Spiritualists, and it was twenty members of this group whom they invited to a private sitting.

The room the Lyons availed for the séance was dimly lit and adjoined a bedroom. Several rows of chairs arranged in semicircles faced the corner of the room where the Holmeses erected a makeshift spirit cabinet out of draperies. As was standard procedure, the most trusted circle sitters sat closest to the cabinet.

One attendee, Mr. H.S. Knight, asked if someone of his own selection could be seated in the bedroom for the entirety of the séance. An obviously irritated Nelson quickly dismissed the suggestion, but Jennie—always the calmer of the two—consented to the arrangement. A man by the name of Lyman Goodrich agreed to solitary confinement in the bedroom, and Jennie's nephew, a man with the surname Gilbert, stood in the only other entrance, a doorway between the sitting room and dining room. Like Goodrich, Gilbert's placement guaranteed, according to Nelson and Jennie, that no one broke the harmonious spiritual discourse once the séance commenced.

Jennie told the circle that she sensed the chances of successfully calling forth the spirits would be greatly improved if they held a "dark" séance, meaning a complete absence of light. Accordingly, the oil lamps were extinguished. Jennie quite quickly fell into a deep trance. Within moments, the sitters could hear bells rolling and falling about the room. Gradually, Jennie's voice slowed and deepened, and she now introduced herself as Rosa, the spirit persona of a Native American maiden.

Taking advantage of the audience's concentration on the medium, circle sitter Pete Miller slowly picked his way to the door beside which Gilbert stood and, claiming exhaustion, leaned heavily against it. He jumped a bit when Jennie—as Rosa—called his name and announced that the spirits had a message for him. She bade Miller to come forward and take her hand. In a whisper indiscernible by anyone more than a few inches away, Miller asked the man next to him to take his place leaning against the door.

Miller navigated the darkened room as quickly as he could and stood before Jennie as she instructed. She clasped both of his hands in hers and proclaimed with great solemnity that—unbeknownst to even him—Pete Miller was a powerful healing medium.

"You must immediately relinquish your position as deputy sheriff and place a shingle out and offer your gifts to the people," said Jennie.

"I'll have to give that some thought," Miller responded before resuming his sentry position at the door.

After Rosa's spirit fully relinquished Jennie, Nelson requested that the lamps be relit. The mediums burst into song, and the jubilant audience chirped along without spurring, for they knew what was coming next. A smiling Jennie Holmes called on Katie King to show herself to the circle.

Heads swiveled back and forth. People shuffled in their seats. The anticipation was palpable. But Katie did not appear.

Jennie and Nelson looked at each other, and fear flashed briefly in their eyes. "Let us sing again," Nelson instructed the crowd. "Let's sing for Katie."

And they did. But Katie King still did not materialize. At least in the front of the room.

Since just before Jennie had summoned Pete Miller, he had been using his full body weight to fend off a now frantic shoving at the dining room door. An angry and resigned Gilbert realized he could not remove Miller from the doorway without betraying his own complicity. He watched helplessly as Nelson and Jennie, oblivious to what was happening at the rear of the room, plodded on.

"Please, Katie," Nelson implored. "These people so want to see you. And we promised that you would be here."

Again the door heaved under the forceful thrusts from the other side, but it was useless. Miller simply refused to budge.

Abruptly the struggle ended, and Miller heard someone run from the adjacent room. By the direction of the footsteps, it was clear the interloper was leaving the house. Miller darted after. He did not realize it, but the runner was taking shelter in the nearest outbuilding, the Lyon family woodshed. It was the closest haven from the men the skeptical Blissfield residents had posted outside the Lyon home to prevent just such an escape. After several minutes in the woodshed, however, panic won out. The door opened, and the fugitive rushed headlong toward the nearest fence.

With only the light of the moon guiding them, the men who ran down and intercepted the fleet escapee thought they had caught a young boy. It was, with some embarrassment, that they realized they were actually— and with great difficulty—restraining a petite woman in men's attire. As she struggled and begged to be released, the gutta-percha cane the woman was carrying (exactly like that usually on the person of Nelson Holmes) snapped in two. After several minutes, the rush of adrenaline subsided, and the woman seemed to accept her capture. Instead of struggling, she tried talking her way free.

She explained to the men that she was merely the hired help. She had been paid by the Holmeses to appear at the séance as Katie King. But, she told them, her real name was Eliza White.

"I'm from Philadelphia," she continued. "My father is a very rich man who would happily reward you if you'll just let me go."

Whether from sympathy, exhaustion or confusion, the men loosened their grip. In an instant, the woman leapt out of their reach, and before the men could regroup, she disappeared behind the neighbor's house. By the time Pete Miller made it to the scene, Katie King was gone.

A crowd gathered quickly, everyone wanting to know what had happened inside the Lyons' sitting room. Miller, whose job it was to catch crooks, easily put two and two together and explained the scam.

"You say she was dressed in men's clothes? That makes sense. Dressed like that, no one would have noticed her slipping into the séance in the dark. Problem is, I wouldn't let her get through the door. If she had made it in she would have pretended to be just one of the guests. With the lights out, she could have gotten to the front of the room without anyone seeing a thing. She takes off the trousers and hat and there you go: Katie King materializes."

The next morning, the unsuccessful captors took a second look at the woodshed and hard-packed soil on which they'd tackled and briefly detained their prisoner. Footprints and skid marks scarred the surface of the dirt. To their surprise, however, another piece of evidence lay out in the open amidst the tracks: the tip of what they were convinced was Nelson Holmes's cane. Emboldened by the find, the party of would-be debunkers banged on the front door of the Lyon residence and demanded that Nelson present his walking stick. Nelson indignantly refused, which only served to further convince the townspeople of his and Jennie's humbuggery. Adding insult to injury, the mediums announced their plans to conduct even more séances in the town. The people of Blissfield were more determined than ever to catch Katie King and this time keep her in their grips.

On September 23, Nelson and Jennie once again prepared the sitting room of the Lyon home for the materialization of spirits. Another small circle of true believers was invited, but for the townspeople gathered outside, the sham was almost too much to bear.

As with all the Michigan séances, the room was completely darkened but this time remained dark far longer than usual. At about 8:30 p.m., after Jennie channeled lesser spirits and after the circle repeated the singing of several songs, the lamps were relit and Nelson Holmes called for Katie King. To his evident relief, she appeared without hesitation but remained visible only briefly.

Katie responded to a second call but again disappeared quickly.

On her third appearance, to the horror of the Holmeses and the few non-skeptics left in the group, a Mr. Frank Brown leapt from his seat and seized Katie in a bear hug. For the second time in a week, the woman worked frantically to extricate herself from a stranger who was equally insistent on keeping her bound.

Within seconds of the grab, Nelson Holmes yelled for the lights to dim, and suddenly the room was swallowed by blackness. This temporary blindness did not prevent the scuffle from escalating into a full-fledged brawl. Peace was only restored by Jennie's nephew's threat to shoot anyone who refused to leave the Lyon house.

And somehow, in the chaos, Katie King once again escaped.

THOUGH THEY HAD successfully evaded complete exposure, perhaps the greatest trick the Holmeses played on the people of Blissfield was their disappearance from the town the next evening. They packed and planned and spoke freely of their next stop in nearby Adrian—but instead boarded a train eastbound, back to Philadelphia, where they assumed no one would ever hear about their disastrous visit out west or the revelations of the woman calling herself Eliza White. Had it not been for little Charley Ross, the news of their Michigan catastrophe probably would have outpaced their return.

Chapter 7
A Long, Sad Fall

JULY 1, 1874, was a clear, hot day in Philadelphia's suburbs. Charley Brewster Ross and his brother Walter were playing in the front yard of their upscale Germantown home when two men stopped their carriage in the street. They were the same men who, just a week before, had given the children candy.

"What's say we take you two boys to buy some fireworks?" one of the men asked.

Without hesitation, Charley and Walter scrambled aboard. "Can we stop for candy on the way?" Charley asked.

"Sure," the driver replied. After halting the horses in front of a small grocery store, he gave each of the boys a quarter. "Buy whatever you want."

Charley took only seconds to choose and purchase his candy. He left the store for the waiting carriage. Walter, far less decisive, wandered around for several minutes before making his selections.

A short time later, a kind passerby stopped to ask the crying child if he needed assistance. "They took my brother and left me here," a sobbing Walter told him.

The abduction of Charley Ross was the first kidnapping for ransom in the United States. The nation wept for Christian Ross as he traveled from state to state to look at countless little boys purported to be his missing son.

Philadelphians were particularly invested in the little boy's story, not only because he was a local child but also because they had in their midst two of the most powerful mediums in the world. Surely Nelson and Jennie Holmes or their spirit Katie King could tell the family where the child was being held. After all, what was the point of communing with the world beyond if the denizens residing there couldn't help the living? Yet, although they knew that every police officer and reporter in the nation was searching for Charley, the Holmeses offered no assistance. Residents of the city, as well as others across the nation, wondered why. "The Philadelphia papers call upon Katie King to tell them something about the Ross child," the *Boston Globe* reported, "but never a word says she."

What had been regarded as harmless entertainment now seemed to many a cruel pit filled with false hope. Editorials in newspapers across the country complained of the conspicuous lack of effort or comment on the part of the Holmeses and other Spiritualist mediums. One editorial from the *Daily Sentinel* in Fort Wayne, Indiana, succinctly summarized the growing consensus:

> *Mind readers and clairvoyants pretend to have powers which might enable them to say where a given person is at a given moment. Charley Ross has been hopelessly lost for several months. His father is crazed with grief and very large rewards have been offered for the discovery of the whereabouts of the abducted child. Strange that no mind reader or spiritualist came forward in that hour of supreme need. Such failure on the part of these gifted people to occasionally utilize their powers gives encouragement to the skeptic.*

With or without knowledge of the Michigan debacle and whether or not they expected word about Charley Ross, by the fall of 1874, covert newspaper reporters and other investigators began infiltrating the séances of Nelson and Jennie Holmes. A *New York Times* correspondent surreptitiously attended a circle and came away with the conclusion that Katie King was one part Spiritualism and two parts humbug. He deduced further that the mediums who materialized her were ignorant and uneducated and theorized that they could not accomplish such sophisticated trickery without assistance. He did admit, however, that at several hundred strong, Katie's circle was a fervent and protective bunch. Perhaps that's why they refused to acknowledge the creaking of wooden boards heard over their singing and why they didn't notice that flower petals in the hallway and on the stairs were strikingly similar to the bouquets circle sitters had earlier presented to Katie King.

Little by little, Katie King's materializations and Nelson and Jennie Holmes's mediumship came under fire from that most powerful force of all: logic. Why were the Katies—American and English—two different ages? One, in London, was a mere child. The other in Philadelphia offered all appearances of a fully developed earthly woman. Why did Katie employ such common vernacular ("I ain't sick, you stupid!") if she was born in seventeenth-century England? Why were many of the items gifted to Katie by admiring circle sitters found in the bedroom adjoining the Holmeses' sitting room? And why were their attendees so scrupulously vetted, with the most loyal always seated in the foremost and most protective positions? People were restless for answers, and Nelson and Jennie Holmes knew that doubt was good for business.

UPON THEIR RETURN to Philadelphia from Michigan, the Holmeses set up residence in a new location, another brick building at 825 North Tenth Street. It was well known that the mediums operated there, and the place was easily found by both believers and skeptics.

Luckily for one self-appointed private investigator, Dr. Lister's antiseptic invention had not yet transmuted into a germ-killing mouthwash. Had Listerine been on the market in 1874, Katie King's Philadelphia career might have lasted far longer.

Chapter 8

And the Fraud Comes Tumbling Down

*Oh, gather round, and let us sing
the praises of sweet Katie King,
who, from her bright and happy sphere,
comes smiling to us mortals here.*

*Then with sweet voices
let all sing
the praises of
sweet Katie King.*

THIS WAS NOT the worst of the songs and poems written for Katie King. Other examples sinned even more gravely against composition, meter and rhyme. But it's the song that became most popular among her devotees and the one the circle sitters sang just before Jennie or Nelson Holmes called her forward to delight the crowd.

As Christmas 1874 drew near, one man—a regular at the Holmeses' Tenth Street séances—developed reservations about the otherworldly status of Katie King. On a cold and snowless night in early December, he picked the familiar path to the circle and, along with the others who he now knew by name, watched intently as Katie King materialized inside her cabinet before stepping out to mingle with her guests.

She was met with the usual cooing and compliments from the audience. "Glorious," said one. "Splendid!" agreed another.

As she touched the hands of the circle sitters, they greeted her with pet names like "Angel" and "Darling." The newly agnostic man waited for his turn to experience Katie King's affection, and he was soon rewarded. Katie leaned close and touched his shoulder.

His withdrawal from her was abrupt and automatic. Her breath, so close to his face, was remarkably foul.

Perhaps this is what the breath of one dead for two hundred years smells like, he tried to convince himself. After a few heart-wrenching moments, however, he knew he must face the truth. Katie King was nothing more than a mortal with bad dental habits. He had been a fool to believe she was anything else.

An old cliché warns that there is no wrath equaling that of a woman scorned. Perhaps a Spiritualist scorned is the one exception to this rule, for the deceived disciple set about demonstrating—with inarguable clarity—the humbuggery of Nelson and Jennie Holmes and their fictional spirit Katie King. He adopted the role of amateur private detective and attended several more séances to take in as much detail about Katie's physical appearance and mannerisms as he could without arousing suspicion. He then started to covertly survey the street outside the Holmeses' apartment.

After several evenings of this undercover investigation, the man noticed a pattern. It appeared that the same woman entered the Holmeses' apartment every evening, well in advance of the start of the sitting, and left only after all the sitters were long gone. Something about her was quite familiar.

With dogged determination, he succeeded in following the woman to a boardinghouse where she regularly took her meals. One afternoon, he stopped in on the pretense of having a meal. To his great pleasure, his quarry was there also, eating alone at her table.

In a gentlemanly and non-threatening fashion, the man struck up a conversation with the solitary diner and slowly, so as not to betray his true intentions, introduced the topic of Spiritualism.

"I don't believe in Spiritualism," the woman quickly replied.

"Oh, nor do I, nor do I," he assured her. But still, there were a couple of mediums who lived nearby and had reputations for doing quite remarkable things, he said.

"Oh yes, the Holmeses," the woman replied. "I went there once. They seem all right."

"Really?" he asked. "Do you think they are genuine?"

Over the course of several days, the man won her confidence. It was as if she welcomed the chance to unburden her conscience, for soon the woman known as Katie King confessed all, including her real name: Eliza White. The same Eliza White caught by the men of Blissfield while trying to escape in male costume.

THE MAN WHO exposed the Katie King fraud had no desire for fame or public gratitude and in fact refused to allow the press to release his name. Before offering his story to a reporter, however, he shared the results of his investigation with Robert Dale Owen and Dr. Henry T. Child. Both were personal friends and both had vouched for Nelson and Jennie Holmes. Without their endorsement, the mediums would never have gained such an impressive audience in Philadelphia.

Owen and Child understood that, even if they went public with their knowledge of the Holmeses' flimflam, many would view it as just another attack on Spiritualism. The only chance they had of shutting the scam down completely was to have the imposter herself confess to her involvement. They were surprised to learn that she was more than willing to cooperate.

The two men retained an apartment similar to that which housed the mediums. In it, they erected a makeshift spirit cabinet. Eliza demonstrated how she materialized and dematerialized using only the dark interior of the space, the shadows cast by the low oil lamps and the power of suggestion. She extended through the black draperies a white hand and then a long, smooth arm just as she had done so many times while Child and Owen watched from the Holmeses' inner circle. She spoke in Katie's signature whisper and exited the cabinet with the practiced finesse that admirers came to imagine was magic. In short, Eliza proved to Robert Dale Owen and Dr. Henry T. Child that every miraculous act attributed to Katie King was a lie.

The extent to which Child was surprised by the revelation of the fraud is arguable. There are many indications that, even if he was unaware of the Holmeses' hoax, he at least had some pecuniary interest in its continued survival. Child, who described himself as "accustomed" to seeing and hearing spirits, produced an 1874 biography of the spirit John King entitled *Narratives of the Spirits of Sir Henry Morgan and His Daughter Annie, Usually Known as John and Katie King.* Rather than actually authoring the tale, however, Child said he served merely as King's amanuensis and that both John and Katie appeared in his office to dictate the book. Immediately after the Holmeses' exposure, however, Child rushed to purchase all unsold copies of his second book, which concentrated solely on Annie Morgan.

Owen was deeply embarrassed and angered by the deception and his unwitting part in it. Perhaps more than anything, he was heartbroken. Like

John King, alias Sir Henry Morgan, "spirit father" of Katie King. From *Narratives of the Spirits of Sir Henry Morgan.*

Child, he realized the only way to mitigate further damage to his reputation was to distance himself from Katie King.

Owen and Child's first course of action was to send notices to the Spiritualist newspaper *Banner of Light.* Wrote Owen: "Circumstantial evidence, which I have just obtained, induces me to withdraw the assurance which I have heretofore given of my confidence in the genuine character of certain manifestations presented last summer, in my presence, through Mr. and Mrs. Nelson Holmes." Child was a bit more succinct, stating simply that he would no longer receive applications to attend the Holmeses' séances, as he now judged the manifestations "unsatisfactory."

While these statements addressed short-term concerns, Owen had a much larger public relations problem. The *Atlantic Monthly* had been publishing a serialized account of his life, and the January 1875 installment was to be one in which he laid out his clear and detailed arguments for the genuineness of the materializations of Katie King. Owen frantically sent word to the magazine begging it to pull the article. Having already gone to press, however, publication of Owen's piece was a fait accompli. To protect its own interests, the magazine did include a letter to subscribers disclaiming both an editorial hand in and accuracy of Owen's work.

Many in the press pummeled the already deflated Owen. "Mr. Owen must find his article in the January *Atlantic Monthly*, which is devoted mainly to Katie, very enjoyable reading about this time," opined the *St. Cloud Journal*, which called the old Spiritualist a "too susceptible believer."

Other publications came to the good man's defense. "Mr. Owen is an earnest believer in the faith he professes," editorialized the *North American and United States Gazette*, "and a man of integrity and culture, so free from guile that the charlatans who make spiritualism a profession for personal gain could readily impose upon him."

Chapter 9
Eliza White Steps Forward

BY EARLY DECEMBER 1874, Philadelphians, like most Americans, knew that Katie King's spiritual manifestations had been soundly debunked. It was one of the biggest stories of the day, and every paper in town spilled substantial ink in covering it. It was an exposé of gigantic proportion—the kind at which Harry Houdini would, several decades down the line, excel. In his 1920 book, *Miracle Mongers and Their Methods*, Houdini revealed the tricks of fire-eaters, sword swallowers and other conjurers and mystifiers. This was resented by many of his fellow magicians, but Houdini was already successful and little bothered by the criticisms of his contemporaries. Four years later (and two years before his death), Houdini took on what he viewed as yet another pack of clever entertainers: Spiritualists.

Early in his career, Houdini had himself operated as a "medium," holding séances for money. After the death of his beloved mother, and upon realizing just how deeply grief cuts and how reverently the dead are held, he regretted that he'd ever engaged in an activity he subsequently said "bordered on crime."

Within days of Houdini's death from peritonitis, the less than subtle subtext of salacious newspaper headlines implied that Spiritualists—if not responsible for his death—certainly felt no sympathy.

We can only speculate as to why Spiritualists reacted more vehemently to Houdini's debunking than did his fellow magicians. Perhaps it was because, as traveling performers, magicians knew there would always be another town with a new audience to trick. Or perhaps they were more realistic about

Harry Houdini was born the same year Katie King appeared in Philadelphia. He would become an enemy of the fraudulent mediums of the early 1900s and expose many of the Spiritualists' tricks. From *Miracle Mongers and Their Methods.*

the lifespan of an illusion. Magicians accepted the fact that eventually the audience would catch on. Spiritualists, on the other hand, were more homebound. They couldn't move on to a new city or theater if their act was outed. Their reputations were local, and their clientele were typically from the immediate surrounds. Exposure of a Spiritualist's chicanery meant the complete disruption—if not destruction—of his or her entire livelihood. But while it makes for a great conspiracy theory to suggest Spiritualists would go so far as to call for Houdini's death, there is no evidence to support the claim.

Like Houdini, Katie King's imposter suffered an outpouring of disdain and attempted intimidation from the Spiritualist community— although the public still did not know her real name. Much of the malice came from the very people who once extolled her praises. Some of it came from her own former employers. In an unsigned letter from Nelson Holmes (whose chirography was identified by Child) written shortly after her private performance for Owen and Child, the following not-so-friendly advice was offered:

> *Before going further in this business you had better consider all the consequences. When once the press takes up this matter, they will make public your past life; certain matters that happened during the war—certain matters that occurred in Connecticut, all of which are fully known and in the hands of those who will make terrible use of them. Why give up a good home and a sure income, and at the same time try and prevent others from getting a living?*

Yet, for all his avarice and willingness to dupe the unsuspecting, Holmes seemed to truly care about how the exposure might affect Robert Dale Owen—or perhaps he just bargained on his confederate being the one with the conscience: "Don't let his death be laid at your door. Tell him you found those 'K.K.' presents and only kept them for mischief, or anything to convince the old man that his past life has not been a delusion and a cheat. Think of his record, his word, and, above all, his mental anguish."

Publicly, the Holmeses fumed at their "betrayal" at the hands of Child and Owen. "If they thought we were practicing fraud upon them why didn't they investigate us?" Jennie asked. "Why didn't they seize the spirit and hold her when she talked to them and shook hands?" Jennie even went so far as to characterize Child as being the Holmeses' business manager. "He paid us $10 or $15 per night and took the receipts at the door," she said.

At the end of December, Robert Dale Owen revealed that he had indeed been investigating the mediums. He dropped one final bombshell about the duo of grifters: Owen learned that just before leaving London for Philadelphia, both Holmeses received checks from a man named Marthese. Each check totaled eight pounds. Before cashing them, however, the Holmeses added zeros, increasing the checks' values tenfold. If nothing else, it proved that neither Nelson nor Jennie Holmes could turn down the prospect of easy money.

NEWS TRAVELED INCREDIBLY fast in the 1870s. There were no fiberoptic cables or high-speed Internet connections, but there were telegraphs, trains and word of mouth. The embarrassing Michigan debacle that the Holmeses hoped would bypass Philadelphia became a syndicated story and nagging nuisance. Still, the mediums successfully deflected most allegations arising from the Blissfield mishap. When the Philadelphia investigation hit the national news wires, however, the scandal became far too large for Nelson and Jennie to manage or spin. The Katie King revelations spread from coast to coast. Reporters as far away as Chicago came to Philadelphia to conduct their own investigations. More secrets about Katie's "materializations" came to light daily. The most explicit details came from the imposter herself, who, in January 1875, offered the *Philadelphia Press* a full confession through which, for the first time, the world came to learn that the spirit Katie King was actually a very mortal single mother from New England.

"I met the Holmeses at a boarding house in Philadelphia," Eliza White explained. "I'm a widow and I was living there with my son and my mother who depends on me. When I ran out of money, the landlady threw me out

on the street. The Holmeses offered to help me if I would work for them."
Eliza, portraying herself as the victim, continued:

> *I was born on the first day of January, 1851, in Massachusetts. I was married between fourteen and fifteen years of age. I have one child, eight years old. My husband died upwards of two years ago, leaving me without any means of support, and through my own exertions I have provided for my child and an aged mother.*
>
> *After my furniture was sold, Mr. Holmes proposed that I should take what little money I had left, purchase as much furniture with it as I could, hire another house, and they would assist me in furnishing it, board with me, and also assist me in paying the rent. I acceded to this proposition. Number 50 North Ninth Street was the house selected, Mr. and Mrs. Holmes using the second floor for their business purposes; the balance of the house, except the store-room on the first floor, was used by us jointly.*
>
> *They commenced giving their pretended spiritual manifestations while we occupied the house on North Thirteenth Street. "Katie King," however, did not make her appearance, for very good reasons, until after we occupied the house on North Ninth Street. This was about the middle of April 1874. Katie King had taken her departure from Florence Cook in London* [and while Spiritualists might be familiar with these events] *outsiders knew nothing about it.*
>
> *One day while conversing…about séances, a white cloth was thrown over my head by the lady medium, accompanied with the remark, "You would make a good Katie King. I wish you would try it. Go in the cabinet; look out at the audience and speak. Say something, just to see how it will take."*
>
> *They offered me two dollars per séance and told me if Katie King caught on they would hold three séances per day. I made up my mind to play the part for a short time, hoping that something better would turn up in my interest. In the meantime I would be earning my expenses and doing no one any harm.*
>
> *All the necessary preparations were made for my debut, which was to take place on the evening of the 12th of May. A robe had been prepared of thin, white French muslin, reaching to the floor, with long flowing sleeves, and fastened around the waist with a belt which, when I put it on, gave me a very graceful appearance. A white veil was then thrown loosely over my head. I had taken great pains to give my face, arms and hands a white, corpse-like appearance. Altogether I looked very much like a spirit.*

Eliza White's discussion of her son and mother never exceeded this casual mention in her confession. This is likely because, wittingly or not, one or both participated in the fraud. Katie King's circle sitters were often astonished to see the arms and hands of a young child appear alongside hers in the spirit cabinet's apertures. Since no records or newspaper reports mention any children in the Holmes household—and since Eliza freely admitted to having an eight-year-old son—it is not unreasonable to assume that the materialized child-like arms belonged to Eliza's progeny.

Spiritualists would raise other doubts about Eliza's statement, but not before she offered a full accounting of her side of the events:

> *I entered the spirit cabinet from the bedroom. Mr. Holmes was already in the cabinet. After one or two false faces had been exhibited, I gently drew aside the curtain hanging over one of the apertures, showing the audience my face, and, in a very low whisper—scarcely audible—said, "Good evening, friends," then drew back my head and threw down the curtain.*
>
> *The sensation in the audience was great. I was amused to hear the different remarks. "Did you hear it speak?" "I wonder who it is?" "How beautiful it was! I do wish it would appear again."*
>
> *Mrs. Holmes told them she knew something unusual would occur, for the spirits had been drawing from her so hard all evening to enable them to materialize that she scarcely had any vitality left.*
>
> *After the excitement had subsided a little I pulled the curtain to one side, showed my face at the aperture, and three or four voices at the same time said, "Who are you? Please tell us your name." I answered in a low whisper, as before, "I am Katie King, you stupid." These were the phrases used by Florence Cook, so Mr. and Mrs. Holmes told me.*
>
> *"Can this possibly be the Katie King who appeared in London?" someone asked. I showed my face again and said, "Of course it is, you stupid."*

Dr. Child then asked the spirit when she last visited London. "I attended a séance there today, you stupid," Eliza replied. Nelson—still in the cabinet with her—signaled that it was time for Katie King to depart, and Eliza sank back into the darkness of the spirit cabinet. Mrs. Holmes asked the circle sitters to sing for the spirit to return. While they rang out in song, Eliza loosened the board on the back of the cabinet, escaped into the bedroom and then ran upstairs to her third-floor room.

The Spiritualists ended the evening on the joyful assurance that the ability of spirits to materialize was a fact now established beyond all doubt.

Chapter 10
No Honor among Spiritualists

ELIZA WHITE, LIKE MANY who confess with self-preservation in mind, laid the Katie King deceit squarely at the feet of Nelson and Jennie Holmes. It was certainly true that they had initiated the fraud, but it was Eliza's performance that generated the bulk of the revenue, and she used this fact to her advantage.

Unbeknownst to their inner circle, in July 1874 Eliza and Nelson had a falling out over money—specifically the amount of money Eliza was owed and paid. Contrary to "Katie's Confession," while her starting salary may have been two dollars per performance, by midsummer it had risen to five dollars per night. Still, however, Eliza and the mediums were sharing the cost of a house, which left the trio dependent on one another. As rumor (and Katie King's subsequent failures to fully materialize) suggested, when Nelson—in one of his well-known tiffs—refused to pay Eliza for July performances he deemed under par, she responded by refusing to perform at all. Likely out of spite, Nelson and Jennie left for Toledo, Ohio, on July 28, two weeks before the August rent came due. To make ends meet, Eliza was forced to pledge some of her belongings to a pawnbroker. But while money may have precipitated the rift, another factor aggravated it: Eliza's imposed confinement. The Holmeses could not run the risk of someone spotting "Katie King" walking down the street, so while they lived at North Ninth Street in Philadelphia, Eliza remained in her room for days on end, only leaving it to perform in the cabinet. This she was no longer willing to endure.

It didn't take long for Nelson Holmes to realize he'd killed the golden goose. Toledo proved a far less welcoming city for the mediums who, bereft of their main attraction, lacked a draw. Shortly after arriving at Blissfield, a desperate Nelson wrote to Eliza asking for her forgiveness for his harsh words. It was just one in a chain of correspondence published after the exposure.

Just over a week later, Nelson wrote again using the now common salutation "Dear Frank." Clearly this was either a pet name or an alias—perhaps a play on Eliza's middle name of Frances. In this letter, he pleaded with her to send newspapers containing stories about the Holmeses and, most urgently, one particular Philadelphia paper that was set to run a photo of Nelson standing beside the materialized "Katie King." If Eliza forwarded a copy of *Frank Leslie's Illustrated Newspaper*, it was likely a request that Nelson regretted. Though the reporters who wrote of one of the Holmeses' Philadelphia séances performed little in the way of investigative journalism, the couple were nonetheless poorly portrayed. Mr. and Mrs. Holmes were, according to *Leslie's*, "two very commonplace persons indeed and of no literary attainments whatever."

On August 28, another letter arrived in Philadelphia from Nelson Holmes, but this time he offered Eliza a more expansive apology and dangled a potential new travel itinerary:

> We have decided on Chicago and will send you a ticket and if we can harmonise [sic] will do better than we did in Philadelphia and try to avoid such foolishness hereafter. I now wish I had let Dr. C. pay the rent for September 15—however, better luck next time. We won't be long in making some money when we once get started again. We will send you your fare from Philadelphia and then, as soon as we can, will pay you back all that you have expended for us and make matters all square again. We will arrange it [in Chicago] that you can go out and come in when you please and enjoy yourself. From there we will gradually work our way back to Boston and remain there [for the summer].

Holmes also instructed Eliza to send her belongings to one Julia Allen in Vineland, New Jersey, although he offered no details on his relationship with the woman.

In his typical pique-ish fashion, Nelson Holmes could not help but complain about the "sapheads" in Blissfield. Performing séances for them, he told Eliza, was like casting pearls before swine—a great irony since it was these "sapheads" who, just two weeks later, would expose the Katie King humbug and prompt the trio to flee back to Philadelphia rather than continue their trek west.

It is interesting to note that never in the correspondence between the Holmeses and Eliza White is a child or destitute elderly mother mentioned. Eliza's quarters are always described as her room—not a shared space—and only one train ticket is offered. Yet in her continuing confession to the press, Eliza lamented over "my helpless little boy and frail old mother looking to me for bread."

"I was alone in a strange city without a home, save the temporary one I then occupied," Eliza said. Was this a slip, or did she neglect to mention them because they lived elsewhere?

"I soon learned how easy it was to deceive the people," Eliza continued. "Night after night was my pillow wet with tears," she said of her guilt. But what of her guilt for abandoning her self-described family? What became of them when Eliza boarded the train to Michigan? The answer likely lies somewhere in the true biography of Eliza White, not the one she fed to the sympathetic reporters in Philadelphia.

WHILE AMERICANS WERE curious as to how a scam as convincing as the materialization of a spirit might be committed, Spiritualists had a far more fervent interest in actually shaping the denouement of the Holmeses' story. The exposure and subsequent confessions were bad for business. The only way to quiet the scandal was to tarnish the reputations of the parties involved.

Henry Steel Olcott—journalist, lawyer, Civil War veteran and special commissioner during the War Department's investigation of the Lincoln assassination—was a recent adherent to Spiritualism who, urged by others in the movement, took up the charge to investigate the Katie King séances. He set out to prove that it was Eliza White who was the true grifter and not the Holmeses, whom supporters now described as trusting mediums fallen victim to a cunning blackmailer.

Olcott, in October 1874, met the famed clairvoyant Madame Blavatsky, and it was from this association that his interest in Spiritualism developed. The two happened upon each other in Vermont, where Olcott was investigating the Eddy Brothers, two siblings who attributed their powers to the supernatural and their bloodline to sorcerers killed during the Salem witch trials. Blavatsky mothered Olcott through his Spiritualist infancy, and in 1875, the two founded the Theosophical Society to advance the study of occultism and other paranormal philosophies. The Holmes controversy was

Henry S. Olcott took it upon himself to repair the reputations of Nelson and Jennie Holmes. From *The Spirit World Unmasked.*

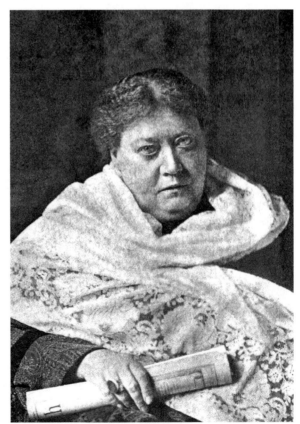

Madame Blavatsky and Henry S. Olcott formed the first Theosophical Society in New York. Blavatsky's 1875 Philadelphia home is today the United Lodge of Theosophists, Philadelphia chapter. From *The Spirit World Unmasked.*

particularly dicey for Blavatsky, who had moved to Philadelphia in November 1874, just before the Katie King exposure. Should these mediums be proven fakirs, it would make followers suspect other mediums as well—perhaps even Blavatsky herself.

Olcott's initial plan was to invite Robert Dale Owen to a private séance to be held under strict test conditions. If Owen could regain trust in Nelson and Jennie Holmes, the episode might fade out of memory with little additional damage. But Olcott arrived too late. Owen and Child had already witnessed Eliza White's Katie King reenactment. So Olcott tried another tactic. Wasn't it suspect, he asked, that Eliza White would confess just when he was coming to Philadelphia to investigate the matter? Either way, Olcott said he was left with no other choice than to reveal her real—and unsanitary—background.

Olcott's inquiry into Eliza White's history was nothing if not committed. There was no mistaking his intent, that being the destruction of the credibility of the faux Katie King. From the ease with which he dug up the dirt, however, it was clear someone was helping him wield the shovel. Within months of the start of his investigation, Olcott's book *People from the Other World* was released by the American Publishing Company. It was divided into two parts, with most of part two focusing on "The Katie King Affair." Olcott relished revealing the name of the secret investigator who broke the story to the newspapers as one W.O. Leslie, who, among other business pursuits, was an original incorporator of the Iron Bank of Philadelphia in 1871. But his strongest vitriol was saved for Eliza White.

"I am sorry to say that an investigation into the personal history of his woman discloses little to her credit," Olcott wrote, "and much to the contrary."

ELIZA WHITE, ALIAS Katie King, was born Eliza Frances Potter in Lee, Massachusetts. Though she "confessed" to an 1851 birth date, she was actually born in 1848. Her father's occupation as stonecutter took the family to Winsted, Connecticut, where Eliza met a man named Wilson Bacon White. He was twenty-five years her senior if census records are correct. In 1870, Wilson and "Lizzie" had a full household in Litchfield, Connecticut, including a seven-year-old boy named Albert and Eliza's fifty-four-year-old mother, Esther Potter. If one assumes that Albert is the son of Wilson and Eliza, it means Eliza was a mere fifteen when she bore him.

Whether Eliza legally married White is unconfirmed, nor has documentation been found to prove her son was fathered by White. What is known about Wilson White is that he enlisted in the Second Connecticut

A drawing of Katie King imposter Eliza White taken from a photograph of her while living in Winsted, Connecticut. From *People from the Other World*.

A drawing of Katie King as she appeared in Philadelphia. Note the similarities to Eliza White. From *People from the Other World.*

Volunteer Heavy Artillery on September 11, 1862, and served as a "junior principle musician" in Company E.

White's company traveled down the Atlantic seaboard before establishing comfortable winter quarters at the District of Columbia. Eliza either joined him there or was traveling with the company the whole time. Whether or not it is as scandalous as it sounds, Eliza "entertained" the men while they wintered and worked as a cook in the officers' mess. After some time, the company was ordered to an active front, and Eliza, according to Olcott, "abandoned herself to a life of immorality in Alexandria."

White served through the end of the war and then returned to Winsted, where he managed a variety entertainment act booked mostly by local county fairs. Eliza, according to the *Waterbury American*, worked the act as a comic singer appearing in "bewitching" costumes, for which the "county swains" poured out their money like water.

In January 1874, the couple's differences turned irreconcilable and Eliza left, taking her son with her. She stopped in Brooklyn, where an uncle gave her money to start a lodging house. She made one more stop in Manhattan before settling in Philadelphia.

Contrary to her confession, Eliza was not a widow, for in fact Wilson White did not die until 1895. And it appears Wilson was a man of some means. At the time of Eliza's decamping, he owned real estate in Connecticut valued at $4,000 and personal property valued at $2,500. Whatever Eliza was running from, it was certainly not poverty. Perhaps she simply tired of sharing a household with a man twice her age. But the larger question is: how did Olcott find this man? No public record exists, and Eliza purposefully hid this information from the press. So who fed him this lead? Olcott's interview with Hosea Allen serves to answer one question and create many more.

"While in Philadelphia," Olcott writes, "I met a gentleman named Allen, said to be a justice of the peace at Vineland, N.J., and as I learn by inquiries made at Lee, Massachusetts, a trustworthy person, who gave me much information as to Eliza's early history." This Allen is in fact Hosea Allen Jr.—husband of the very Julia Allen to whom Nelson Holmes instructed Eliza to ship her furniture.

It is unlikely that Olcott's introduction to Allen was coincidental. Nelson and Jennie Holmes had more to gain from Olcott's book than anyone, so they undoubtedly connected these dots for him. But how, then, did the Holmeses come to know the Allens?

Like Eliza, the Allens originally hailed from Massachusetts. Julia was born in Lee just nine years before Eliza White. Could the Holmeses have met

Eliza in New England long before they set up shop in Philadelphia? If not, it must be assumed that it was by sheer luck that Nelson Holmes met both Julia Allen and Eliza White—two women from the same town in Massachusetts, both living in or near Philadelphia in the late 1870s.

In his sworn statement to Olcott, Hosea Allen said that he was a school supervisor in Lee between the years 1842 and 1857. Eliza attended this same school, he said, having first enrolled there in 1846. At this time, Allen asserts, "she was about six years old." This would make her even six years older than the census records document, a bit unlikely when one considers how youthfully she was described by those who got the closest look at her. As for Eliza's character, "Her moral reputation was," said Allen, "as bad as it could be."

Allen admitted that he visited the Holmes household on North Ninth Street in Philadelphia in June 1874 and in fact stayed for two days, although he gives no reason for being there. It was at this time, he said, that he first learned of Eliza's presence in Philadelphia. Coincidentally, Allen also met Dr. Child during his visit. Child's purpose for being there was, according to Allen, to supervise the construction of the walnut spirit cabinet from which Katie King appeared. In one final damning surprise, Allen said he was in the house during a circle sitting and—while Katie King was materializing— Eliza White could be heard humming and singing on the floor above. It was proof, according to Allen, that Nelson and Jennie Holmes were the truthful parties in the relationship and powerful mediums to boot.

Owing to Olcott's goals for his book, he never investigated Hosea Allen's background or veracity. Had he done so, he would have learned that Hosea Allen never offered his occupation as "justice of the peace," nor do any New Jersey records indicate he was one. In 1870, Allen calls himself a "grocer" and in 1880 a "shipper of fruit." His 1883 death record describes him as "retired." Why a man of means, as Hosea Allen seemed to be, would defend so passionately Nelson and Jennie Holmes is a mystery, but that he did is quite clear.

Like criminals who without remorse give up confederates to save their own skin, Henry Olcott cast aspersions against anyone who might aid in the exposé of his Spiritualist community. Incredibly, his book and campaign to rehabilitate Nelson and Jennie Holmes—and, by association, Spiritualist mediums across the nation—worked. At least in the short run.

Chapter 11
Smoke and Mirrors

Oh, where is Mr. Owen now?
Where has that false, false lover strayed,
Who used to praise this bonny brow
And say my face
Was full of grace?
Alas, that I should be betrayed!

Because I was not made of gas,
Of emanations, and such things,
But honest rags and looking-glass;
And dresses old
Did me enfold,
And 'cause I had not real wings.

My cruel lover jilted me,
And called me false, and could not see
That under rags and jags may be
The liveliest ghost
That ever crossed
The dingy Acherontic sea.
—*"Katie King's Lament," from* The Graphic

IT IS ONE THING to watch a magic show and laugh as someone else is
tricked. It is another when the trick is played on us.

The circle sitters who turned up night after night to watch the materializations of Katie King—whether or not they thought she was a spirit—still wanted to know what *really* happened in those séances. Many of them accepted the fact that they had been fooled, they just wanted to know how. Like many of the best illusions, the key was simplicity.

When, for instance, skeptical invitees to the Ninth Street sittings wanted the adjoining bedroom door kept open—the door through which Eliza White accessed the spirit cabinet—Jennie Holmes opened the séance by channeling a message from the spirits: "The light is interfering with our manifestations." Lamps were blown out, enveloping the room in blackness, and Eliza White simply descended from the floor above and entered by the same door the sitters had used. Any noise created as she surreptitiously entered the cabinet was drowned out by the bells the "spirits" tossed about the room, the musical instruments spirits loudly played or the hymns Jennie insisted attendees sing over and over again.

Exiting the cabinet at night's end was surprisingly easy. To the delight of the Holmeses' sitters, the deep, mysterious voice of Katie's father, John King, rumbled forth from the depths of the cabinet, "I am here. If you put out the lights, I may muster enough strength to materialize." To this the attendees eagerly agreed. Once Eliza scampered from the back of the cabinet and out the parlor door, Jennie made the sad announcement. "I'm sorry," she told the disappointed crowd. "The conditions were not right. John King has gone."

If guests demanded to thoroughly search the bedroom before Jennie locked its door, an even more ingenious—yet equally simple—tactic was employed. The Holmeses' bed was outfitted with a second mattress substantially longer than the one underneath. The lower mattress was pulled away from the headboard, and a bamboo cage filled the empty space. The longer top mattress covered the entire contrivance. Eliza White, well in advance of the sitting, crawled inside the cage. When the bed was made, no evidence of the deceit was visible. Anyone pushing down on it would find it firm from head to foot. When visitors finished their examinations, Jennie secured the door to bar further access. To achieve Katie King's materialization, Eliza only had to crawl out of the cage and enter the cabinet through a dummy board in the rear wall. Anyone viewing the panel assumed it was solidly secured. In truth, the screws made no contact with the cabinet's frame.

Getting back inside the bed took far more time than crawling out of it, which is why, at the close of every séance, there was always a ten-minute period when Jennie Holmes attempted to make contact with the spirits without retort. "I'm sorry, they have gone," she would announce when she was confident Eliza was tucked safely back under the mattress.

When Katie King peered from the lower cabinet aperture and then, seconds later, smiled out of the higher hole some six feet above the floor, believers accepted the Holmeses' claims of levitation. In actuality, Eliza had only stepped onto a stool covered in black cloth, making it invisible in the dim light, even when the cabinet door was open.

The spirit writing that so impressed Robert Dale Owen was a base forge-and-swap. Like Owen, Nelson Holmes also studied Frederick Robertson's handwriting—only Holmes did so well in advance and for the sole purpose of copying it. Both Holmes and Eliza were in the cabinet for this trick, and she explained it in one of her confessionals:

> *The letter was written by Mr. Holmes, who had a fac-simile of Robertson's handwriting in the house. When the blank paper was passed into the aperture another sheet, on which the lines had been inscribed, was substituted and the paper…was held on a black board by Mr. Holmes who had on a pair of black gloves. I then drew over my right arm a black covering, leaving only the hand and part of the wrist exposed. This presented the appearance of a detached hand, and with the pencil I pretended to trace out the words on paper.*

As for all those faces peering out of the cabinet—all the dead siblings, parents and grandparents habitués swore they recognized—most were nothing more than rubber masks that could be stretched to suit nearly any facial oddity or expression. Nelson tucked a dozen or more India rubber faces inside his pockets before he entered the cabinet. The rest were hidden in the dark recesses where, whether by faith or ignorance, the circle sitters failed to look.

When the trio moved to Tenth Street in the fall of 1874, the spirit cabinet was positioned in front of a window shielded by closed exterior shutters. Inside, the window casing had been removed. Panels were added to the sides of the cabinet, increasing its depth and making it look like it had been built into the window recess. In actuality, Eliza White hid between the exterior shutters and the back wall of the cabinet, entering it through the same dummy board she'd always used.

Katie King's dematerialization at the end of each evening was perhaps the most rudimentary trick of all. While sitters gasped in astonishment, Eliza slowly lowered a mundane piece of black gauze fabric over her face while stepping backward toward the darkest corner of the cabinet. To devotees, it seemed like magic. In actuality, it was an optical illusion that any bright child given a dark room and enough cloth to hide behind could accomplish.

In a rare display of skepticism, Dr. Child once questioned Jennie Holmes about her young boarder whom he had spotted leaving the building one afternoon. She bore a striking resemblance to Katie King, Child observed. His suspicions were quickly dampened, however, when one evening, shortly after the séance ended, the home's doorbell rang fiercely and repeatedly. Jennie rushed to answer, only to find her tenant loudly complaining of being locked out every time the Holmeses held a sitting. Child, who witnessed this dramatic event, apologized for insinuating collusion between this obviously innocent young woman and the mediums.

THE REGULAR ATTENDEES who had been so easily hoodwinked by Nelson and Jennie Holmes were just a small fraction of the vast number of men and women throughout the ages who succumbed to the spell of artful jugglery (the practice of using sleight of hand with the intent to deceive). The most astute of men can be hoaxed, as even Harry Houdini learned. Before he became a magician of legend, Houdini's hero—and the reason why he became a conjurer—was French performer Robert-Houdin. Although Robert-Houdin claimed sole authorship of the remarkable tricks he performed, Houdini eventually learned that Robert-Houdin had filched most of his act from his predecessors. Even his "autobiography" was not Robert-Houdin's but, rather, the work of a French journalist. Houdini felt his only course was to expose his former eidolon, and he did so in his book *The Unmasking of Robert-Houdin*. There is a passage on the last page that, while written of Robert-Houdin, could just as well have been about Nelson and Jennie Holmes and other late nineteenth-century Spiritualist mediums:

> *The master-magician, unmasked, stands forth in all the hideous nakedness of historical proof, the prince of pilferers. That he might bask for a few hours in public adulation, he purloined the ideas of magicians long dead and buried, and proclaimed these as fruits of his own inventive genius. That he might be known to posterity as the king of conjurers, he sold his birthright of manhood and honor for a mere mess of pottage…and juggled facts and truth to further his egotistical, jealous ambitions. But the day of reckoning is coming.*

Chapter 12

Owen Breaks

THE YEAR 1875 was a troubling one for Spiritualism and Nelson and Jennie Holmes in particular. London's "Katie King"—real name Florence Cook—was caught, shivering and in a state of partial undress, in her spirit cabinet within weeks of the publication of the American Katie King's confession in the Philadelphia press. As if Eliza White's statements were not damning enough for Nelson and Jennie, in March a Philadelphia carpenter named John Trainer filed an affidavit saying he had been hired by the Holmeses to create their spirit cabinet. Trainer admitted the end product was nothing more than a theater prop meant to fool the audience and described how Nelson Holmes instructed him to create the movable boards to allow access through the cabinet's rear wall.

Germantown's Charley Ross was still missing, prompting ever nastier and more sarcastic calls for the Holmeses and their spirits to assist in his recovery. The Steubenville, Ohio *Daily Herald and News* ran one such item: "A Memphis, Missouri, medium reports little Charley Ross 'all hunk in Paradise.' He's happier there where Katie King can show him all the nice things Mr. Own gave her."

Paris's Katie King was not just exposed but prosecuted. Using costumes, rubber masks and fake scenery, three enterprising individuals had been selling "spirit photos" to sitters who were delighted to see Katie and other spirits hovering near and around them in the developed shots. They charged only twenty francs per photo, but some grateful customers gave as much as four hundred. The two Frenchmen involved in the plot were sentenced to one year of confinement each. The American female assistant received a lighter sentence of six months.

Madame Blavatsky, the theosophist who publicly disparaged the Holmeses, was now facing her own exposures and was described in one District of Columbia newspaper as "a superb charlatan."

If Nelson and Jennie Holmes were truly remorseful about deceiving Robert Dale Owen, the saddest news came in July 1875, when headlines across the nation—some sympathetic, some searing—announced that Owen had lost his mind.

Like any good son, Ernest Dale Owen tried to protect his father's reputation. He was not insane, Ernest assured, nor was his breakdown a result of the Katie King affair. Yet, on July 9, Robert Dale Owen was admitted to the Indiana Insane Asylum—only six months after the Holmeses' fraud was detected and publicized.

At first the Owen family blamed the breakdown on physical causes. Robert Dale Owen had suffered an attack of bilious nervousness recently, they said, and it taxed all of his faculties, including those of his mind. Later came the revised story that Owen was writing a new book on theology and underestimated how much it would take out of him. He was, after all, a man in his seventies.

Owen's behavior was not violent nor was it particularly irrational. But he could not stop his mind from attempting to work out issues invisible to others. He fired off decisions and pronouncements with hectic rapidity. He demanded to go to New York; moments later, he demanded to go to Philadelphia. He told his children he was building them all large estates complete with fine carriages and servants. He declared himself the last surviving family member of the first Earl of Breadalbane, although there was no evidence to support the claim. He was restless and couldn't sleep or eat, and only movement seemed to soothe him. Said Ernest of his father's calmness while riding in a carriage, "He seemed to think he was accomplishing something because he was going somewhere."

Owen did not speak of Katie King in the weeks leading up to his confinement in the asylum, and the family refused to allow the subject of Spiritualism to be discussed in his presence. "He was very much chagrined," Ernest said, "and thoroughly indignant at the deception."

Time and time again the family insisted that Robert Dale Owen's derangement had nothing to do with Katie King or Spiritualism. When Owen's daughter, Rosamond, joined in the public denial, many could not help call to mind Shakespeare's admonition: the lady doth protest too much.

Katie King is parodied in a political cartoon. From *Frank Leslie's Illustrated Newspaper.*

WHILE ROBERT DALE OWEN struggled to regain his sensibilities and dignity, Nelson and Jennie Holmes struggled to convince Spiritualists that Katie King was still materializing at their séances. "She has only been able to materialize her hands and face," Jennie told inquiring sitters. "But she will fully materialize soon."

Seeking to escape the figurative and literal heat of summer in Philadelphia, Jennie Holmes traveled to Brooklyn in August 1875. Nelson was not with her, perhaps due to the same illness that had several times previously absented him from the sittings. Jennie had accepted the invitation of the Society of Spiritualists that was offered, ostensibly, in response to Jennie's published call for aid after the Katie King exposé. But before they would vouch for or assist her, the society said, members wanted proof of her mediumship.

The members of the Society of Spiritualists were so anxious to see the Holmeses' materializations for themselves and to aid in Jennie's demonstration that they even went so far as to erect a spirit cabinet to her exact specifications. For six consecutive evenings, Jennie Holmes was scheduled to provide exhibitions of her mediumistic powers at the society's hall on Fulton Avenue.

Although the venue was new, Jennie's script was not. As always, she told the audience she would begin the evening with a "dark" séance. She did add one new wardrobe item, however: a large sack made of lightweight muslin, which she stepped into and shimmied up over her body. She then asked one of the society's members to tie it securely around her neck. Other members of the audience were called forward to inspect the unusual confinement prior to assisting Jennie's entrance into the cabinet and found it to be a common, though quite oversized, fabric bag with no apparent means of escape. To their surprise, shortly after sealing Jennie inside the spirit cabinet, arms and faces appeared in the apertures, one face none other than the long-dead pirate John King. When he faded away, Katie King took his place. She whispered invitations to several men and women to come forward and touch her. Soon thereafter, she melted away, back to spirit land.

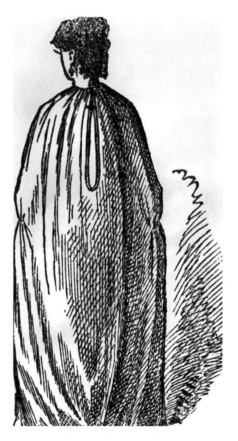

Some members of the Society of Spiritualists wondered if they had judged Jennie Holmes too hastily. The second night of Jennie's séances, however, proved far less impressive. As she had done the night before, Jennie materialized Katie King, who again invited audience members forward for closer inspection. This hubris proved Jennie's downfall, for

Jennie Holmes voluntarily allowed circle sitters to tie her inside a large bag to prove she had no hand in the materializations at the Holmeses' séances. From *People from the Other World*.

on this night she was careless. A woman approaching the aperture noticed that two locks of curls—suspiciously like Jennie's—dangled against "Katie's" forehead. Her announcement of this observation prompted a full-scale investigation of Jennie's cloth bag. As with all of the Holmeses' tricks, the solution was elementary and easily discovered once attendees knew where to look. One thread used to bind a seam was left unknotted. Upon entering the cabinet, Jennie simply pulled it out of the fabric, leaving a hole of a yard or more through which her arms and hands could operate freely.

Though discretion would surely have been the better part of valor for Jennie, she continued to give séances for four more nights. Each succeeding night, the audience grew more hostile. One attendee demanded to hold Jennie's hands during her dark séance. She adamantly refused, using the old chestnut about "proper conditions." Another attendee wanted to pin Jennie's bag closed—a request that was also denied. Through it all, Jennie continued to "materialize" Katie King, who sometimes stood upright, other times appeared on hands and knees and once appeared crouching.

At the sixth séance, the novelty of Jennie's dishonesty wore thin. One gentleman wondered aloud why the spirit of John King emitted no breath while Katie King could be heard and felt exhaling warm air. Other men in the front row insisted that the faces of John King and other spirits were nothing more than rubber masks. They demanded that Jennie allow several women in attendance to search her person.

Realizing that she was outnumbered and outmaneuvered, Jennie's only recourse was flight. In dramatic fashion, she recoiled from the crowd. "Oh my," she said, "I think I might faint!" Jennie asked where she might sit for a moment and then tottered unsteadily out of the room. Members of the Society of Spiritualists were amused to see the fainting spell suddenly lift when Jennie reached the stairs where her hat and shawl waited. Apparently now perfectly recovered, she bolted to the door and out into the street. Even an offer of $100 was insufficient to induce Jennie to return to the hall and finish her exhibition. It was, therefore, the final opinion of the Society of Spiritualists that Jennie Holmes was a fraud.

Like cats, Nelson and Jennie Holmes seemed to shed one life and start anew on another while their detractors followed in relentless pursuit. During one dark séance, Jennie announced that the guitar music the sitters enjoyed was produced by a spirit. A skeptical visitor lit a match, providing enough light for the circle to catch Jennie holding the instrument over her head and plucking at its strings.

Spirits take control of a medium's guitar and tambourine during a séance. From *Confessions of a Medium*.

Members of another sitting thrilled to the possibility that Katie King had finally returned in full materialized form. "Good evening, friends," spoke the face at the aperture—and this time it was clearly no rubber mask.

"Can you step out of the cabinet, Katie?" Jennie asked.

After several attempts, a female form stepped forth, only to quickly disappear back inside.

It was the editor of the *Philadelphia Evening Bulletin* who broke the disappointing news. Using the opera glasses he'd smuggled into the séance, the newspaperman was able to discern that the sitters had not seen Katie King but rather Nelson Holmes dressed in women's clothing.

IN EARLY OCTOBER, much-needed good news reached Robert Dale Owen's family and friends. The superintendent of Indiana's hospital for the insane announced that his most famous patient could return home. Although more rest was advised, Owen was deemed capable of resuming all of his former work and activities. Owen wrote a letter of appreciation to the doctor in which he also expressed gratitude to those members of the press who had treated him and his family kindly during his affliction.

The year 1875 brought good tidings to one other person as well. While impersonating Katie King may have brought Eliza White notoriety and scorn, it also opened her eyes to a new career. The woman who brought Spiritualism to its knees announced she was studying for the stage.

Chapter 13

Strike a Light

That peculiar form of ghostly circus known as the "materialization of spirits"
has lost much of its popularity in consequence of the indiscretion of the now
disgraced spirit Katie King, who loved onions not wise, but too well.
—New York Times

WITHIN A YEAR of Eliza White's confession, nearly all of the best-known mediums in the nation had been exposed as fraudulent, albeit talented, conjurers.

Mrs. Mary Hardy, the medium who foretold Robert Dale Owen's meeting with specters, had long been revealed as a grifter. A cunning, self-appointed debunker liberally dusted himself with carbon powder before attending one of her Boston sittings. At the end of a dark séance during which "spirits" repeatedly caressed and patted the sitters in attendance, the lamps were relit. Mrs. Hardy and numerous members of her circle found themselves blotted with black smudges. It was an embarrassment from which she never recovered. She died just two years later at the age of thirty.

Anna Eva Fay, equally well known in both London and America and another of Sir William Crookes's "proven" mediums, was convicted in New York on charges of jugglery. The presiding magistrate ordered her to obtain a juggler's license or go to jail.

Dr. Henry Slade was a medium who supposedly channeled written spirit messages via a contraption constructed of hinged school chalk slates. He made a comfortable living from his deceit for quite some time, but

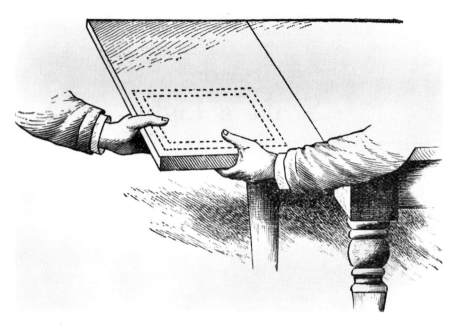

One example of how mediums perpetrated their slate-writing fraud. From *The Spirit World Unmasked.*

earnings diminished after investigators replicated the trick. Depending on his surroundings and ease of concealment, Slade either swapped out blank slates for those with pre-scribed messages, or he used a small piece of chalk tucked under his fingernail to scribble the words while unsuspecting clients waited for the reveal.

It seems his own cons were insufficient to satisfy Slade, however, for he also publicly vouched for other swindlers. One of his unsavory alliances included a man calling himself Dr. J.D. MacLennan. MacLennan would travel the country, advertising "free treatment for the poor, while the rich are expected to pay a moderate fee." He reportedly cured patients of afflictions ranging from sinus pain to rheumatism, deafness to paralysis. The four-month paralysis in question was suffered by none other than Dr. Henry Slade, who offered a (likely paid) testimonial describing Dr. MacLennan's ability to restore the use of his limbs in "less than twenty minutes."

The Davenport Brothers were, perhaps with the exception of the Eddy family of Vermont, the best-known mediums of the late 1800s. Tied inside a specially outfitted cabinet that accommodated the both of them, the audience was assured the men were incapable of moving let alone playing the various musical instruments locked in the cabinet with them. Yet, as

The Davenport Brothers (and their spirit cabinet) were some of the most popular nineteenth-century mediums. From *The Spirit World Unmasked*.

soon as the cabinet doors closed, sounds of guitars and tambourines rang out. Like the Eddys, the Davenport Brothers attributed their powers to the supernatural. Toward the end of his life, however, Ira Davenport confessed to Harry Houdini that the act was an elaborate fraud effected by slipknots and invisible wires and that neither he nor his brother ever believed in Spiritualism.

Many Philadelphians had long since chalked up Spiritualism, mediums and materializations as nothing more than artful and entertaining bamboozlements. They were therefore shocked to learn that Nelson and Jennie Holmes had returned to the City of Brotherly Love—and to their old and now laughable tricks.

The nomadic couple took an apartment on Locust Street in the area today known as Washington Square. Only the most fervent believers attended the

Holmeses' séances now. More numerous were the skeptics who hoped they, too, could achieve their fifteen minutes of fame by catching the mediums mid-hoax.

Regardless of the number of times the Holmeses had been publicly proven disingenuous, one man—Dr. J.M. Roberts of Burlington, New Jersey— refused to relinquish his faith in them. Roberts's son, by contrast, viewed the couple as criminals preying on his father's susceptibility.

On a bitter night in February 1876, several dozen curiosity-seekers braved the conditions and traveled to the Holmeses' ill-lit and unheated parlor. Self-preservation now dictated the seating arrangements, and Jennie was careful to place doubters between believers. She blew out the lamp, slipped into a trance and, in a squeaky impersonation of a child's voice, said, "Good evening, friends." When someone in the circle jingled a bell in an attempt to startle Jennie out of her supposed catatonia, Nelson lit a match to identify the offender. It would have been better had Nelson ignored the interloper, for Jennie immediately took his bait. Trance imitation forgotten, she loudly berated the man and, in doing so, did his debunking for him.

Gullible Dr. Roberts was incensed by the intrusion and disruption. Recognizing the trickster as a newspaperman, he demanded the reporter be ousted. When his request was ignored, Roberts indignantly left the séance.

Jennie, now determined to maintain control, told the sitters to hold hands. "If the person beside you tries to pull away or relax his grip, tell Nelson to strike a light," she instructed.

Jennie once again slipped into her "trance," but the crowd would have none of it. Once again, she broke out of character to scold the audience, and they responded with rowdy insults.

With some effort, Jennie was able to herd the audience out of her parlor but not before collecting seven fifty-cent stamps from seven newspapermen.

Nelson was of no help in disbanding the group, for he had barricaded himself inside the spirit cabinet.

J.M. ROBERTS'S DISDAIN for reporters began when they started using his name in articles about the Holmeses' connection to the Katie King fraud. He filed suit against the editor of the *Philadelphia Times*, claiming libel, and vehemently defended himself against stories that made him look foolish and feeble. His testimony before the magistrate, however, did little to convince the court that he had complete control of his senses. When asked how often he attended Nelson and Jennie Holmes's séances, Roberts replied, "Every night but Saturdays."

The star witnesses in Roberts's defense were none other than Nelson and Jennie themselves. Nelson (who was subpoenaed as James N. Holmes) testified that he never charged Roberts or anyone else admission but rather only accepted gifts from satisfied sitters. Jennie was next to be called and strutted toward the witness box in a stylish suit paired with one of her signature matching hats. To her surprise, the defendant (acting as his own lawyer) announced he had no questions.

"I am sorry to hear that," a playful Jennie responded with mock disappointment.

"Come back," called the defendant. "I will hear you."

"Our fee is fifty cents," she said, contradicting her husband. "This gentleman here," Jenni said while pointing to a *Times* reporter standing close enough to touch, "still owes me money. He gave me his card, but I can't eat or drink that."

Chapter 14

Philadelphia's Bliss Diminished

Robert Dale Owen died on Sunday, June 24, 1877 at his summer home at Lake George. He was elected member of the Indiana legislature, served in the House of Representatives, introduced the bill for the organization of the Smithsonian Institution, represented this country at Naples for five years—but he is best known by his writings, especially upon Spiritualism, in which he was a sincere believer. He was an earnest seeker after truth and his spirit of fairness won the respect of all, even when he was plainly mistaken.

ROBERT DALE OWEN never erased the stain Spiritualism left on him. Every obituary and eulogy made some mention of it; most pointed out that his faith was deluded. After his death, observers tried once again to link the collapse of his mental and physical health to Katie King. One final time, those closest to Owen repeated that the old man's energies had simply been depleted by the work he seemingly never suspended. If the Holmeses made comment on Owen's passing, it was not made public.

Nelson and Jennie were dealing with their own struggles in 1877. While visiting Vermont in late summer, they were thrown from their carriage and badly injured. In a somewhat cruel news report, the *St. Johnsbury Caledonian* suggested that "some of our people think it will be no great loss if they are unable to humbug the people for quite a while to come." By the end of the year, both had recovered, however, and resumed holding séances. The couple spent two weeks in Washington, D.C. Initially, they stayed in one home and performed the séances in another, but Jennie explained this considerable loss of magnetism adversely affected the chances for spirit manifestations. Other circles were simply too large, said Jennie, and the Holmeses could only call forth one indistinct form. Once the mediums were able to reside and conduct séances in the same house, the materializations succeeded. Jennie's now well-known spirit control Rosa made a number of appearances. Dick appeared in voice only. Spirit lights bounced around the room, as did musical instruments borne (in the dark) by unknown forces. It was a friendly audience—the first Nelson and Jennie had met in weeks—and one of Nelson's last reported sittings.

Why the mediums spent the summer in the nation's capital is debatable. Perhaps the invitation was too good to refuse. Or perhaps they wanted to get out of Philadelphia, where another Spiritualist scandal would have only opened the scars left from their Katie King scam.

James A. Bliss was a con man who abandoned his wife and children in Boston in favor of a pretend marriage to a Spanish woman named Christiana. He used the suffix "Dr." and called himself a magnetic physician. His wife described her talents as "full-form materialization."

Shortly after arriving in Philadelphia, a spirit photographer named Thomas Evans asked James and Christiana's help in expanding his business. Evans's own wife and daughters often appeared in his fraudulent photos, and he was looking to add new talent and expand his enterprise. Bliss agreed to the partnership and moved into a building at 1027 Ogden Street. Evans arranged for construction of a spirit cabinet accessible from the basement beneath via a connecting trapdoor. Sitters would have been shocked to learn that the hinges were concealed only by the wood trim at the base of the cabinet front. Had a curious visitor tugged at the tacked strip, Bliss would have been caught far earlier. His downfall came not because of sitters' suspicion, however, but because of a skeptical member of the press who was now familiar with—and expecting—Spiritualists' tricks.

When the journalist overheard the medium speaking of a need for repairs to the pipes in his basement, he seized the opportunity and convinced the plumbers to allow him to enter the cellar with them. There, completely unprotected from view or inspection, was the wooden ladder by which mediums accessed and exited the spirit cabinet, a large collection of costumes and wigs, stage makeup and powder and copies of the Spiritualist publication *Banner of Light*. Bliss was caught red-handed, and there was no escaping to another city to avoid the consequences. He was tried for conspiracy to defraud and theft by deception, but the jury failed to reach a unanimous verdict. The Blisses retreated to Boston, where they continued with séances and materializations. Mrs. Bliss complained that the people of Philadelphia had been so vile and slanderous that it nearly made her give up on her calling as a "messenger for the angels." But after the death of her husband, she returned to the city and, unfortunately for Christiana, was well remembered by the police. On the signal of an undercover officer, police crashed her séance to find Christiana "materializing" a male spirit through aid of men's attire and fake whiskers. The crying girl clinging to the medium's leg was heartbroken to learn this was not her grandfather after all. Christiana was hauled before the magistrate to answer charges of conducting a disorderly house, a catch-all crime that meant allowing any number of unsavory activities to proceed unabated under one's roof. Mrs. Bliss disappeared shortly thereafter.

IT IS IN 1877 that the last mention of Eliza White is found. A small item repeated in newspapers around the country provided the final detail: "The woman who impersonated Katie King in the Philadelphia materialization séances has gone on stage. She appears in a play called 'Katie King; or, Spiritualism Exposed.'"

Where the play was staged, or where it folded, is not known.

Chapter 15

Spiritualism Rises from the Dead

THE THIRTY-EIGHTH ANNIVERSARY celebration of the founding of Modern Spiritualism brought the Holmeses, Katie King and the Fox sisters full circle. Although Spiritualists organized events and programs nationwide, it was the First Brooklyn Society of Spiritualists that boasted the headliners.

When society president Mr. Waterman abdicated master of ceremony duties due to a death in the family, none other than Jennie Holmes replaced him. We can only wonder if it was with relish or regret that, on March 28, 1886, she called Maggie and Katie Fox to the stage. The sisters took their seats at a table and immediately began rapping. But the demonstration was brief.

Mrs. Holmes explained to the audience that the Fox sisters were tired from their day's labors and that, as spirit communications depended so much on their mediums' physical condition, no more could be heard that evening. "The good spirits have gone now," she announced. "If we stay any longer we will be overrun by spirits with whom we may not care to be en rap-port."

Just two years later, Maggie appeared at New York's Academy of Music to declare that there never had been anything to Spiritualism at all. It was, she confessed, all a ruse. This confession devastated many whose faith in Spiritualism was born of their faith in her. "I am now eighty-one years old and have but a short time of course, to remain in this world, and I feel great anxiety to know through you if I have been deceived," one man wrote. But even facing the backlash from believers and her fellow mediums, Maggie was defiant. "I was the first in the field," she said, "and I have a right to expose it."

In 1888, Jennie Holmes suffered one final public exposure. She was grabbed mid-manifestation during a dark séance in her home in Unionville, New York. In the harsh glare of the relit lamps, there was no fooling the sitters into believing they were seeing a spirit rather an aging conjurer whose audience had finally deciphered her tricks. Where and when she and Nelson died and are buried is unknown.

Dr. Henry T. Child passed away in his Northern Liberties home in June 1890. His obituary mentions his charitable work, his service helping the wounded at the Battle of Gettysburg and his part in forming the Universal Peace Union. There is no reference to his involvement with Spiritualism.

Katie Fox died suddenly on July 4, 1892. Though the newspapers said she was fifty-three, she was actually fifty-seven. Maggie never recovered from the loss. Eight months later, she died at the age of fifty-nine. The woman on whose shoulders the banner of Spiritualism was most prominently lifted exited the mortal realm destitute, childless and homeless. Only the kindness of a few old and faithful friends saved her from dying in the street.

The University of Pennsylvania honored Henry Seybert's requests and created a commission to study Spiritualism and other supernatural activity. The list of

Dr. Henry Slade was one of the best-known slate-writing mediums of the time. From *The Spirit World Unmasked.*

mediums tested reads like a who's who of the movement in the nineteenth century: Maggie Fox, Dr. Henry Slade, Harry Kellar, Fred Briggs and others. In the end they reached the conclusion Seybert least desired: the so-called manifestations were not caused by spirits but rather (more or less) successful sleight of hand and deception on the part of the mediums.

"It has been said," H.H. Furness Jr. wrote in the commission's report, "that Superstition is, in many cases, the cloak that keeps a man's religion from dying of cold; possibly the same may be said of Spiritualism."

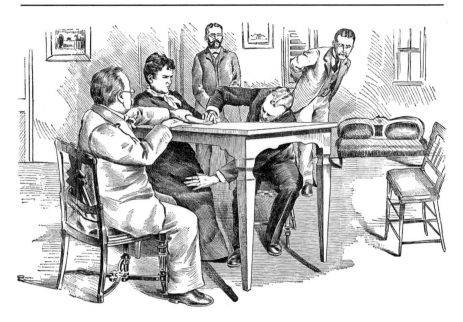

Scientists search a medium to ensure no tricks are employed during the séance. From *The Spirit World Unmasked*.

"[I have] found fraud where I looked for honesty," Furness concluded, "and emptiness where I had hoped for fullness."

At the movement's fiftieth anniversary celebration, F. Cordryn White, event host and leader of the Milwaukee Society of Spiritualists, claimed more than ten million Americans adhered to the theology. Attendance at the commemoration seemed to contradict him, however, for fewer Spiritualists than ever came to this annual celebration. Still, White assured, "The Spiritualist colony is anticipating an awakening of interest in its work."

Ironically, considering the number of fraudulent mediums who had recently and persistently suffered public exposure, the five-day gala ended with a masquerade ball.

MOST ASSUMED THAT by its fiftieth anniversary, Spiritualism, already fading, would finally recede into the pages of history—that it would become one of those quirky chapters in man's past that, while entertaining, bore little importance. And this likely would have been the case had it not been for World War I.

Like the Civil War before it, the war to end all wars sowed in its bloody furrows the seeds of fear, anger, confusion and doubt. And, as during the previous conflict, those burying their loved ones sought reassurance of an afterlife.

Strong, famous surrogates for the movement now included Harry Houdini's friend Arthur Conan Doyle, who lost his own son in the First World War. So open was Doyle's mind to the power of the supernatural that he refused to believe Houdini when the magician assured Doyle his tricks were not the product of spirits but rather old-fashioned cunning and legerdemain. The silly tiff turned into a bitter feud, and the two men publicly harangued each other for the remainder of their lives.

During Spiritualism's brief renaissance in the early 1900s, the Fox cottage was moved from Hydesville to Lily Dale, New York, a community of mediums that still exists today. The building was destroyed by fire in the fall of 1955. There is a lush, shaded meditation garden where the cottage once stood. The original commemorative plaque remains in the ground: "Memorial to the Fox family who lived in this cottage at the time Margaret and Katie Fox, aged 9 and 11 years, received the first proof of the continuity of life, which was the beginning of modern Spiritualism, March 31, 1848."

Dozens of registered mediums live and work in Lily Dale. Due to an overwhelming number of requests for readings, appointments are highly recommended.

Sources

Blavatsky, Helena Petrovna. *A Modern Panarion: A Collection of Fugitive Fragments.* Vol. 1. London: H.P.B. Press, 1895.

Cadwallader, Mary E. *Hydesville in History.* Chicago: Progressive Thinker Publisher House, 1917.

Campbell, Rev. John Bunyan. *Spirit Vitapathy.* Cincinnati, OH: H. Watkin, 1891.

Carrington, Herward. *The Physical Phenomena of Spiritualism, Fraudulent and Genuine.* Boston: Herbert B. Turner & Co., 1907.

Child, Henry T., MD. *Narratives of the Spirits of Sir Henry Morgan and His Daughter Annie, Usually Known as John and Katie King.* Philadelphia: Hering, Pope & Co., 1874.

Confessions of a Medium. New York: E.P. Dutton & Co., 1882.

Cowles, Hon. George W. *Landmarks of Wayne County, New York.* Syracuse, NY: D. Mason & Co., 1895.

Crookes, William. *Researches in the Phenomena of Spiritualism.* London: J. Burns, 1874.

Daniels, J.W. *Spiritualism versus Christianity.* New York: Miller, Orton & Mulligan, 1856.

Davenport, Reuben Briggs. *The Death-Blow to Spiritualism.* New York: G.W. Dillingham, 1888.

Davies, Rev. Charles Maurice, DD. *Mystic London or Phases of Occult Life in the Metropolis.* London: Tingley Bros., 1875.

de Heredia, Carlos Maria. *Spiritism and Common Sense.* New York: P.J. Kennedy & Sons, 1922.

Doyle, Arthur Conan. *The History of Spiritualism*. London: Cassell & Co., Ltd., 1926.

Elder, William. *Biography of Elisha Kent Kane*. Philadelphia: Childs & Peterson, 1858.

Evans, Henry Ridgely. *The Spirit World Unmasked*. Chicago: Laird & Lee, 1897.

Facts. Vols. 2–3. N.p.: Facts Publishing Co., 1883.

Hare, Robert. *Experimental Investigation of the Spiritual Manifestations*. New York: Partridge & Brittan, 1855.

Hearst's International 39 (January 1921).

Houdini, Harry. *A Magician Among the Spirits*. New York: Harper & Bros., 1924.

―――. *Miracle Mongers and Their Methods*. New York: E.P. Dutton & Co., 1920.

―――. *The Right Way to Do Wrong: An Exposé of Successful Criminals*. Boston: Harry Houdini, 1906.

―――. *The Unmasking of Robert-Houdin*. New York: Publishers Printing Co., 1908.

Hull, Rev. Moses, and W.F. Jamieson. *The Greatest Debate within a Half Century Upon Modern Spiritualism*. Chicago: Progressive Thinker Publishing House, 1904.

Jewett, Pendie L. *Spiritualism and Charlatanism: The Tricks of the Media*. New York: S.W. Green, 1873.

Lillie, Arthur. *Madame Blavatsky and Her Theosophy: A Study*. London: Swan Sonnenschein & Co., 1895.

―――. *Modern Mystics and Modern Magic*. London: Swan Sonnerschein & Co., 1894.

Lippitt, Francis J. *Physical Proofs of Another Life, Given in Letters to the Seybert Commission*. Washington, D.C.: A.S. Witherbee & Co., 1888.

Mahan, Asa. *The Phenomena of Spiritualism*. New York: A.S. Barnes & Co., 1876.

McCabe, Joseph. *Spiritualism*. New York: Dodd, Mead & Co., 1920.

Olcott, Henry Steel. *Old Diary Leaves: The True Story of the Theosophical Society*. New York: G.P. Putnam's Sons, 1895.

―――. *People from the Other World*. Hartford, CT: American Publishing Co., 1875.

Overland Monthly and Out West Magazine 16, no. 93 (September 1890).

Owen, Robert Dale. *The Debatable Land between This World and the Next*. London: Trübner & Co., 1871.

―――. *Footfalls on the Boundary of Another World*. Philadelphia: J.B. Lippincott & Co., 1860.

Page, Prof. Charles G., MD. *Spirit-Rappings and Table-Tippings Exposed*. New York: D. Appleton & Co., 1853.

Popular Science Monthly 42 (1893).

Preliminary Report of the Commission Appointed by the University of Pennsylvania to Investigate Spirituality in Accordance with the Request of the Late Henry Seybert. Philadelphia: J.B. Lippincott Co., 1920.

Richmond, A.B., Esq. *What I Saw at Cassadaga Lake: A Review of the Seybert Commissioners' Report.* Boston: Colby & Rich, 1890.

Sargent, Epes. *Proof of Palpable Immortality.* Boston: Colby & Rich, 1875.

Tuttle, Hudson, and J.M. Peebles. *The Yearbook of Spiritualism for 1871.* Boston: William White & Co., 1871.

Space constraints prohibit the listing of every one of the hundreds of newspaper articles consulted while researching this book. Suffice it to say, however, that the facts and contextual details offered by these stories provided an immeasurable understanding of the birth and growth of Spiritualism and its effects on both the believers and skeptics. What follows is a list, organized by state, of the most pertinent publications on which the author relied.

CALIFORNIA
Los Angeles: *Daily Herald*
Oakland: *Evening Tribune*
San Francisco: *Daily Evening Bulletin*

DISTRICT OF COLUMBIA
National Republican

HAWAII
Hawaiian Gazette

ILLINOIS
Cairo Bulletin
Chicago: *Inter Ocean*
Decatur Republican

INDIANA
Clarksville: *Weekly Chronicle*
Fort Wayne: *Daily Sentinel*
Logansport: *Daily Star*
Logansport: *Weekly Journal*

IOWA
Atlantic Telegraph

KANSAS
Atchison Daily Champion
Dodge City Times

MAINE
Bangor: *Daily Whig & Courier*
Camden: *Herald*

MASSACHUSETTS
Boston: *Daily Globe*
Boston Investigator

MINNESOTA
St. Cloud: *Journal*

MISSOURI
St. Louis Globe-Democrat

NEW YORK
Frank Leslie's Illustrated Newspaper
New York Times
Utica Daily Observer
The World

OHIO
Cleveland: *Daily Herald*
Freemont Weekly Journal
New Philadelphia: *Ohio Democrat*
Perrysburg Journal
Stark County: *Democrat*
Steubenville Daily Herald & News
Tiffin Tribune

PENNSYLVANIA
Philadelphia Bulletin
Philadelphia Inquirer

Philadelphia: *North American and United States Gazette*
Ridgeway: *Elk Advocate*
Titusville Morning Herald

SOUTH CAROLINA
Orangeburg Times

VERMONT
Rutland: *Daily Globe*

WISCONSIN
Eau Claire: *Free Press*
Janesville: *Gazette*
Milwaukee: *Sentinel*

Index

About the Author

If you include her first poem published by the *Hummelstown Sun*, Stephanie has been working as a published writer since the third grade. Traditionalists, however, would likely say that Stephanie's professional writing career began in her twenties, when she was hired as a stringer by the long defunct *Pennsylvania Beacon*. Since that time, she has amassed more than two hundred bylines in local, regional and national publications. Her previous book, *The Killing of John Sharpless: The Pursuit of Justice in Delaware County*, was released by The History Press in April 2013.

A lifelong Pennsylvania resident born within smelling distance of the Hershey Chocolate Factory, Stephanie specializes in topics relating to history, true crime and folklore.

Stephanie lives in the capital region of the state with her husband, two dogs and two cats (the brains of the operation). When not writing or researching for editors or paying clients, she writes and researches Hauntingly Pennsylvania, her own history site, for free.

Stephanie enjoys hearing from readers, so feel free to contact her via her website, StephanieHoover.com.